For Bill

my favorite pastor
and good friend of
many years. With
esteem.

Bob

June, 1980

The
Examined
Life

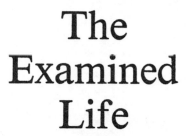

The Examined Life

by
Robert E. Burns

THE THOMAS MORE PRESS
Chicago, Illinois

ISBN 0-88347-121-3

Contents

Foreword

THE writings you hold in your hand and are about to read are quite out of fashion. Out of fashion, not old-fashioned. If they were old-fashioned, they would find their clientele among nostalgia buffs and others who would like to repeal change. No luck for you, if you crave membership in such a clientele. *The Examined Life,* while it by no means enjoys all forms of change, recognizes that in church and world change is here to stay. With Richard Hooker, the author knows that all change is inconveniencing, including change from worse to better. But welcoming the possibility of something creative in change does not make this book fashionable.

Let me hold you in suspense about the out of fashion character of this book by pointing first to three subsidiary remarkable features about writing that looks all too modest to state its own claims. Then, point four will state my claims.

First, it is remarkable that columns written by an editor on page two of his or her magazine are worth gathering into a book. (And you will find them of worth. Truth in packaging laws are operating in the present instance. The publisher quite properly feels that here is a worthwhile exception to the rule that editorial ruminations are best left on the ash heap of ruminators past). Some of my best friends are

editors. Some of the best editors treat "their" page
the way I used to treat the last three inches of space in
our parish church bulletin. A secretary would come
in and say, "Pastor, we did not quite fill the issue.
People won't mind something from you. Why not
dash something off?" And I would join a great
company of clergy dashers-off in writing grayish and
blurry copy that parishioners knew it did not pay to
read and that even I would doze over while proof-
reading.

Not so with "the examined life" columns. I do not
know whether Bob Burns crafts them or whether they
come by inspiration from divine spirits, but they do
not merely take up editorial space. It is impressive to
see that, while most of them are tagged to identifiable
past events, they live in the present. Somehow they
still nudge us or make us perk up.

Now for a second remarkable feature. The author
knows how to make a distinction between the
examined life and the over-examined life. The
unexamined life, we have been told, is not worth
living. The over-examined life, you are now being
reminded, is not living in the first place. Many
examiners over-burden their readers with scrupulous
self-scrutiny. Their readers have to traverse all the
theories of psychoanalysis and all the fashionable
therapies before they come to the point. And the
point is usually that under all our psychoneurotic
layers there are deeper psychoneurotic layers, and
that through the primal scream or the experience of

8

the Holy Spirit or whatever we are supposed to cope with them and then transcend them. No such bad luck here.

As Burns examines life he offers the never really in fashion analysis and therapy we call common sense. Common *sense* because he relies on a measure of experience of the ordinary. *Common* sense because as Catholic and humanist he draws on the inherited and almost intuitive wisdom of greater and lesser people who have beat him and us to the starting line so far as examination of life is concerned.

Now for a third remarkable feature and it is a third reason to see *The Examined Life* as not being in fashion. In fashion are highly focused obsessions. One author has as her shtick the notion that if Roman Catholicism will start letting homosexual women marry each other and then be ordained we will finally grope our way into the kingdom. Another is sure that if you would only follow him in picking up the wisdom of the peyote-chewing members of the Native American Church the true meaning of the eucharist would emerge. Still another is fashionable enough to parade a fanaticism for some liturgical reform, and repeats editorial comment on it as often as you repeat liturgy. It is fashionable to become known for one cause, one specialty. Editor Burns and his magazine are devoted to examination of the life of the U.S. Catholic, and have come to recognize that that life is full of competing interests and conflicting impulses, each of which have to await their turn.

Since the author's writing is of that character, it is in place for me, the publisher's invited guest on these front pages, to be a bit obsessive and fanatic about a single theme: that the out of fashion columns here remarkably bid for your attention.

And now for the fourth point, the one that really stamps *The Examined Life* not as old fashioned but out of fashion. The tone of voice and the spirit behind them is civil. And civility has been a sufficiently rare virtue that it was never quite in fashion. Most of religious history has seen people kill in the name of faith. They have felt righteous about their crusades and empires, triumphalist about their achievements at the expense of the competition, certain about their rights to live the unexamined life.

Those days of incivility are not gone forever. The ayatollahs of Shi'ite Islam, the killers on both sides in the Asian sub-continent, the Middle East, northern Ireland, and much of Africa, use the names of gods and religions to justify their bloodthirst. Closer to home the Christian Voice of the Moral Majority joins Catholic bumper-sticker sloganeers in wishing death to the someone or other who disagrees with them. Only the fact that there are so many competing kinds of slogan-shouters and the fact that pluralist America does not find them all gathered in one region or hollow keeps us from seeing them enact their murderous rages.

So what else is new? What else is new is that some humanists, academics, and theological cheer leaders are taunting them on or us to join them. Civility is out of fashion in a day when the aggressive churches grow, the belligerent attract clienteles, the militants draw headlines. If you are civil, goes the common wisdom, you cannot have or express conviction. Conviction in religion is murderous, say unbelievers and overbelievers alike. If you *really* believe, I hear some agnostic colleagues urge, you would kill—as did the Inquisitors, the Crusaders, and Conquistadores, and other saints of the past.

No, says Bob Burns in column after column. The conviction is there, but as he has examined life it is clear that he believes one can have what Quakers call "convincement" but can blend it with empathy and responsiveness. "Oh, I see your point," Burns often seems to be saying of his opposition (and he has opposition). But then he tries to get them or the resistant us to see his.

Neither the publisher nor the author and certainly not I believe that a book like this will make a big difference in the world. Other publishers have louder megaphones and bigger promotion budgets and many if not most other authors can toot and trill their trumpets better than Burns. But as with much out of fashion writing of a civil sort, this collection is less directed toward utopian and messianic expectations than to the simple need to give voice to what is in a thoughtful person and an often apathetic community, in this case Catholicism, a community with a potential for being stirred. The truly civil author has faith that there is something intrinsically valuable about the examined life. It may not lead to conquest or the end of troubles. But its absence makes the world a bit more cruel, much more cold, and certainly less habitable. Here's to civility, *The Examined Life* style, a toast too rarely raised, but never more in order than now and here.

Martin E. Marty
Fairfax M. Cone Distinguished Service Professor at The University of Chicago, associate editor of *The Christian Century,* editor of *Context.*

Sex Education Belongs in the Gun Store

THE widely celebrated film, *The Deer Hunter*, whatever its flaws, is a strangely disturbing movie. It isn't the kind of film that one watches and forgets. Most viewers, I suspect, will find themselves thinking about it from time to time in the ensuing days.

The director/writer of *The Deer Hunter* has used two recurring symbols to construct a kind of theme for the movie: guns, particularly handguns, and sexual inadequacy. Handguns, contrasted with the rifles used in the idyllic hunting scenes, are thrust at the viewers again and again in tortured and tortuous games of Russian roulette. And all of the principal male characters are shown as being sexually inadequate in one way or another.

In the calm light of the day after, the viewer is likely to realize that the acceptance of the torturers' demand to play Russian roulette was far more dehumanizing and ultimately cowardly than facing the alternative. But in the intensity of the drama's presentation of the dilemma, the opposite seems true. Gambling with one's life, over and over again, seems to be the *macho* thing to do. The filmmaker obviously found a correlation between the sexual inadequacy of the principal men in his story and their exuberant willingness to use handguns even when such use jeopardized their lives. "Forget about my

13

sexual hangups," they seem to be saying. "Watch me handle this gun. You'll see how masculine I am."

I make this point because these two themes seem to run as threads in our American way of life, too, intertwining at many key intersections. A high incidence of, at least, concern about sexual inadequacy is a mark of contemporary American culture. I doubt that any civilization has given jobs to as many "sex counsellors" as has ours and vast industries in clothing, cosmetics, entertainment, media, and automobiles (!) are built and marketed by appeals to the gnawing fear of countless sexually insecure Americans.

I don't suggest that the prevailing condition I have described is limited to Americans. Nothing of the sort. But it may be more pervasive in the United States than anywhere else today. It also, I think, seeks a remedy, particularly among American men, that is unique. The remedy, of course, is the strange American love affair with handguns.

For a long time there was a tendency to explain the American fascination with guns by referring to American frontier history. All the men on the frontier carried side arms, we were told. And today countless Americans still believe that there is something un-American, unred-blooded about Americans who dislike guns. But this notion of American frontier history has since been proved false. Most frontiersmen did indeed own guns, for hunting food and

occasionally for self-defense when travelling over-
land. But nearly all those who carried side arms, including most of the legendary gunslingers, were out-
laws of the most detestable type. Most showdown
shoot-outs, we now know, ended with someone shot
in the back. But the myth persists, propagated continually by fictional films and TV dramas.

There isn't room here to further psychoanalyze
American gun fascination. But its obsessive nature
among many Americans needs to be noted. It needs
to be noted because one opinion poll after the other
shows that Americans overwhelmingly favor (70% in
one recent poll) strict control of handguns, and yet
the minority will prevails. It needs to be noted
because nearly all American police officials favor—
sometimes plead for—handgun control to reduce the
scandalous number of homicides committed with
handguns, and yet the minority will prevails.

The minority, it appears, is able to make its will
prevail not only because it is extraordinarily well
organized but also because many of them are fanatics
who sincerely believe, in the depths of their psyches,
that handguns are good in themselves. I am convinced that many of the arguments they advance in
support of complete freedom to own handguns are
mere, after-the-fact, window dressing. The true gun
lover cannot believe that anyone needs reasons for
owning guns. One need only ask why the typical gun
lover can never be satisfied with owning a *single* gun

or need only observe a gun lover inspecting, loading, unloading, cleaning, oiling, fondling his guns. Embarrassing!

We Americans are, in many respects, an unusually civilized people. But we will never be able to celebrate our emergence from barbarism until we learn to control guns and our far too pervasive love of them.

Let's Put Women in Their Place

WHEN Pius XII was Pope he seemed to be tireless in receiving groups of every kind. One day it would be Alpine mountain climbers or American basketball players; the next it would be Belgian lace makers or Spanish olive pressers. I remember that on one occasion he gave an audience to a group of Roman bus drivers and in his remarks to them he admonished them not to cheat when making change for their passengers. Speaking with a friend who had lived in Rome for years, I expressed my sympathy for the Pope. "The poor man," I said, "must be at his wit's end trying to think of something to say to all the varied groups." My friend saw it differently. "It was very important for him to say that," he told me, "the Roman bus drivers cheat like mad."

I thought of this while skimming through some of the numerous statements that Pope John Paul II is making to numerous groups. Like the President of the United States, everything he says, if not news, is at least grist for the media mills. And like the President, he must depend on the help of assistants to write statements for him to deliver on the many, varied occasions that confront him.

I have taken the trouble to write this preamble because I would like to think that the remarks spoken by the Pope on the role of women were written by someone else. Not that I am suggesting that the Pope would speak words that are contrary to his views—and in this instance his views were consistent with those often uttered by Catholic officialdom. It's just that I would be more comfortable if I could believe that the views expressed were not deeply felt, from the heart.

Speaking to women gathered for the 10th National Congress of Italian Domestic Workers (!), the Pope said that "domestic work must be seen not as an implacable and inexorable imposition, as slavery, but as a free choice, conscious and willing." If he had stopped there, no one could seriously quarrel with him but he added, "which fully realizes women's nature and fulfills their needs." Now that, I respectfully suggest, is nonsense.

If you tell me that by tradition, by education, by acculturation, or by fiat, woman are more likely or more accustomed to domestic work than men, I will agree. But no one has ever presented a shred of evidence that women are of their natures inherently more suited to domestic work. It may even be true that in a society organized differently than ours, the male of the species might have the responsibility for "maintaining the home" (while women worked outside) and do a better job of it than women do now.

If the Pope's words had been spoken by a U.S. senator from Pennsylvania or by the Prime Minister of Luxembourg, I wouldn't be bothering to write about them here. I do because I fear that they reflect a conception of women that is so wrong that it is enfeebling the church. I don't believe that ordaining women to the priesthood is crucially important—although denying ordination to qualified women is rather weird—but somehow a way must be found to bring the life experience of women to bear on *all* levels of the church. I can think of no other way to remedy the truncated conception of women that is reflected in this statement of Pope John Paul. In a world stuffed with problems that no people has ever faced, so sophisticated that they threaten to burst the very seams of our existence, a church that is more than half female cannot afford to limp when it must walk boldly.

A Pope has, of course, every right to express his views publicly on any subject although the address to the Italian domestics was surely not a matter of faith or morals. I am reminded, too, of the distinguished designer of church buildings who began a meeting with a bishop who had contracted for his services by pointing out, "In matters of church architecture, Your Excellency, it is you who is the layman." But a benighted understanding of women on the part of church leaders is bound to be pervasive in innumerable areas of religious life.

Is it too much to ask that every Catholic, from the Pope to the least member of the community, humbly wipe the slate clean of unexamined presumptions inherited from another era and invite representative women and men in proportion to their numbers in the church to meet early and often for the purpose of spelling out the fair place of women in the church? That, I think, would be little enough.

Can Christians Short-Circuit Power Gone Mad?

FOR years my barber has been telling me that life in our so-called civilization is controlled ultimately by something called "the system." The system, as he sees it, is neither a hoodlum empire like the Cosa Nostra nor a stacking of the laws of statistical probability toward an inevitable outcome. It is a little of each and more. Its practical outcome is that it leaves almost all of us powerless to make any substantial change in the way we live.

I have never really argued with John, not only because I don't like the odds when he alone has the sharp instruments, but because I've found it hard to take his theory seriously. I still do but I'm increasingly less sure that there aren't more than a few grains of truth in what he preaches.

Just the other day, for instance, the head of the Tennessee Valley Authority warned that "the life-blood of the country is in the hands of a few people who have more power than the government." A former federal energy adviser, S. David Freeman, documented his agency's claim that "the price of uranium—and thus, indirectly, the price of much of the nation's electricity—is set by a concentration of giant energy conglomerates that controls the price and production of several types of fuel." By way of illustration, he pointed out that since 1970, the price of coal has risen from $5 a ton to $25 and of uranium from $9 a pound to $40.

A day or two later, the Union of Concerned Scientists charged that the nuclear power plant terror in Pennsylvania should not have come as a surprise. The UCS said it had documentary evidence of more than 150 instances in which atomic power safety recommendations had been overridden by career bureaucrats in the Nuclear Regulatory Commission. All but a relative handful of us haven't the foggiest understanding of nuclear power and that handful with some degree of scientific sophistication, it seems, are locked out of sufficient understanding by a few who invoke security to cover their blunders.

The system? Is it so unreal after all? Is it possible that despite our rightly vaunted freedoms, the growth of an overweening technology and the increasing concentration of power in a few hands is making Americans (and citizens of western and other democracies) as powerless finally as the citizens of a Latin American banana republic dictatorship? Are we so drugged by the swollen inventory of material possessions which most of us enjoy today that we don't realize that we really can't do a damned thing about the runaway inflation that has brought corporate profits to a few and $100 grocery carts to the many?

Pope John Paul II singled out our embarrassment, not of riches, but of possessions as the subject of his first encyclical letter. He sharply criticized the "consumer civilization," arguing that we must not become "a slave of things, the slave of our own products."

And both the Pope, at Puebla, and the Latin American bishops assembled there, called strongly for Catholics—and all people of good will—to place themselves unmistakably on the side of the powerless. I make this distinction because most Americans with their "middleclass" incomes can hardly be described as poor. Yet increasingly they are becoming powerless. Our democratic political processes remain essentially unchanged but money now looms so important in conducting media blitz campaigns and too many of us have become so show-biz-sodden that a successful candidate must be both richly endowed and more entertaining than the Tweedledee he or she opposes.

How, it is reasonable to ask, can Catholics place themselves effectively to redress the imbalance of power that exists? I doubt that many of us want a wild-eyed ayatollah with threats of amputations, kangaroo courts, and firing squads (although there might be a moral in the shock and surprise of the now deposed Iranian ruling class). And faithful readers know that I am not enthusiastic about advocating specific legislation or even social action from our altars.

But we have in the statements of recent popes and those of many church leaders abundant material for homilies that are indeed religious. Pope Paul VI's letter, "The Progress of People" may have been the

Robert E. Burns

most important and at the same time least known statement of a church leader in this half of the 20th century. Concretely illustrated by down-to-earth situations confronting all of us, this letter could provide the stuff of a dozen meaningful homilies.

To wit: How many congregations would continue to doze as they often do if a homilist began by asking, "How much did your groceries cost this week?"

You're Nobody Till Somebody Gives a Damn

THE mass suicide of "cultists" in Jonestown, Guyana, was as puzzling as it was horrifying. How had the leader of this strange quasi-religion persuaded more than 900 of his followers to swallow poison as they did?

Obviously, Reverend Jim Jones did not gain his power to persuade his followers overnight. They had become accustomed to following his directions over a period of time during which they repeatedly subjected their wills to his. As the story of the cult unfolded in the days following its self-inflicted holocaust, we learned that this bizarre colony was financed in large part by social-security and other governmental benefits that Jones had persuaded the hapless victims to sign over to the group through him. Nearly all of the victims were poor, most were black, and in signing over their meager benefits they had given up all that was between them and destitution, starvation, and perhaps death. Far from clutching their last few dollars with a death-lock grip, they appeared to have given these away gladly. Why?

At a conference sponsored by the Anti-Defamation League, 25 scholars from a variety of disciplines tried to answer this question. Not all of them followed the sage advice of sociologist Marvin Bressler of Princeton University. Bressler commended those of the participants who expressed "some degree of humility in trying to understand (the cult phenomenon) rather than issuing pronouncements at this point." But he also spoke of those at the meeting who had tentatively suggested that Jonestown may have represented the "exhaustion of the doctrines of secular salvation."

If this latter suggestion has merit, it would seem to affirm the frequently heard belief that there is a pervasive hunger today for the spiritual, the metaphysical, perhaps even the religious. And there is abundant evidence that more than a few "doctrines of secular salvation" have been tried and found wanting. Our still almost unquestioned faith that universal education would make the world little less than a paradise is one of those exhausted doctrines. Our not always expressed but widely held assumption that a high standard of material well-being would cure what once ailed us has also let us down. Ideological alternatives to rampant capitalism such as Marxism have turned sour in the mouths of their adherents and the yellow-brick road that the neo-Freudians beckoned us to follow them down to adjustment and inner serenity led more often to Times Square at the rush hour.

Without at all looking down my nose at this theory and with due respect for Bressler's warning to approach so complex a puzzle with "some degree of humility," I offer a far more mundane explanation

for the willingness of the Jonestown people to sur-
render their wills to that of another. Unlike the
membership of some of the cults flourishing today,
the Jonestown people were neither affluent nor
drawn from the cultural or racial majorities. On the
contrary, they seem to have been people whose lives
were bleak and empty. They apepar to have been
people the world passed by. Nothing of consequence
happened to them; the biggest thing in their week was
probably the next episode of "Charlie's Angels" or a
copy of *The National Enquirer* discarded on a
crosstown bus. They were nobodies. Nobodies until
Reverend Jim Jones came along and told them they
were somebodies.

Jim Jones was a clergyman of a mainline denom-
ination and it's not unreasonable to assume that at
one time he sincerely wanted to help others, to lead
them in the ways that Jesus lived and taught. If that
is true, how sad it is that he could not have used his
ability to make nobodies realize that they were somebodies without using this insight to twist and exploit.

How sad, on the other hand, to see countless people, some clerical, some lay, of flawless integrity and
unlimited goodwill who lack the warmth to reach out
to the nobodies all around them. Austere in their
lofty residences, they proclaim unquestionable truths
and wonder why it is that more than a relative handful don't make the pilgrimage to their doors. How
sad that these good people don't come down from

their aeries to extend their hands in warmth and friendship to countless people who need and want that so much.

When we evangelize from the top of a hill, we shouldn't be surprised if most of what we say goes over the head of many.

Grandma and Grandpa Never Had It So Good

IF you are looking for a profound-sounding statement to make at a social gathering, one that is guaranteed to bring a maximum of head-nodding agreement, try saying, "The American family is disintegrating." But if you do, breathe a silent prayer that no one replies, "Just what do you mean by that?"

It's the conventional wisdom that the family "is in trouble" but no one seems too sure what this means. The family, of course, is a catchall because everyone obviously belongs to one. So every social malaise short of nuclear war is ascribed to family breakdown. But a few problems, legitimately called family problems, seem to be those most often mentioned. The divorce rate, teenage and especially unmarried pregnancies, couples living together without marriage, abortion, and a variety of offenses grouped under the pitifully inadequate term, juvenile delinquency.

These problems have one thing in common: They have all been with us for many generations. Some of them have increased in number but even these instances bear examination. Divorce, for example. There are certainly more divorces in America than there were 10, 20, or 50 years ago. But their number has been increasing steadily over that entire period and there is even evidence that the rate of increase has flattened out in recent years. To this should be added the fact that divorces are generally much easier to obtain than previously.

The prevalence of divorce in our society is surely a cause for sadness. But saying this is not to deny that there are divorces and divorces; that among many divorces of convenience or selfishness, there are some at least that bring an end to the mating of hopelessly incompatible or irremediably immature partners.

The incidence of unmarried couples living together has probably increased in our day but no one really knows. It may simply be that there is much greater openness than there once was or greater availability of suitable places to live together. (Art Buchwald once mused that the throbbing movie, *Last Tango in Paris,* was really about the housing shortage in Paris.)

It is probably also true that teenage pregnancies and those outside of marriage have increased numerically. But here too comparisons may not be what they seem. The dramatically earlier onset of puberty in girls and greater openness may be significant factors. Unmarried pregnant girls are far less likely today to visit Aunt Mildred in another city.

It is, I believe, the widely held image of the family that has changed far more drastically than the family itself. For a substantial number of Americans, maybe the vast majority, the family is a well-scrubbed, faultlessly coiffed, radiantly healthy couple with two or three children cut from the same cloth. Mom meets Dad at the commuter train station in suburbia in a squeaky-clean station wagon or van from which the children and a dog with a bandage on his foot wave and wag. In this wonderful world of Norman Rockwell there is no room for deviation. (What, after all, is lower than a deviate?) There is something vaguely wrong about an unmarried son or daughter who wants to live away from the family unless, of course, they are away at college. There is something vaguely wrong about a son or daughter, at home or away, who remains unmarried "too long."

One painful result of this last hang-up is the fact that countless bachelors of both sexes are involved in anything but rewarding marriages because marriage is expected of them.

The wife and mother of the family is expected to be multitalented and splendidly self-sufficient. She must be well dressed, well groomed, well read, and charming but, most important, must know her place! She should, *par excellence,* be the woman in the beer commercials who carries in the tray of bottles and glasses to the men, then gets out of their way. (Have you noticed how only an occasional waitress, waitress-wife, or camp follower ever appears to mar the all-male fun in the many TV beer commercials?)

It ought to bother us a little, I think, that this image of Total Woman fails to allow for the fact that more than half of the women in the United States are employed outside the home.

I don't think I have exaggerated in describing the image of the family that many if not most Americans hold. And I suggest that the variations from this idealized picture that abound today are inaccurately seen as symptoms of family breakdown. Some of the symptoms I've mentioned are indeed signs of illness or weakness in our society but as I've pointed out, they're hardly new. Other "symptoms" are not that at all, merely variations from the rigorously stylized family portrait that hangs in the galleries of many minds.

Some of the things that were good enough for our grandparents ought to be good enough for us. But other things that in retrospect seem to have been all warm and right for them may not be good for us today. And who knows, maybe they weren't all that great for Grandpa and Grandma either.

Armageddon Anyone?

IT'S almost as if the American people were Stoics or fatalists. But I don't think we are. A happier explanation would be that, as a people, we have a deep and abiding trust in God and his providence but I don't see any reason for believing that either. Nonetheless, there has to be some explanation for the lethargy with which we greet the news that, in dozens of areas, we are on a collision course with disaster.

I recall a description of the planet Venus which has come for the first time within our "orbit." Believed to be completely sterile and utterly incapable of supporting our kind of human life, Venus is a planet much like our earth in size and in some other attributes. And there is an at least plausible hypothesis that Venus was once very much like our world, supporting life as does ours until environmental trauma of one kind or another destroyed this capability. Still I'm not optimistic that we will respond to this warning with any real effectiveness.

When we are told, for example, that our present way of life may very well lead to the destruction of the ozone layer that shelters us from the ultimately annihilating infrared rays of the sun, we tend to ask "How soon?" If the answer is, "By the year 2050," we will, more than likely, shrug and reflect that we won't be around that long. If this were a scene from a *cinema verite* film, the camera would then pan to an infant lying happily in its crib.

We are willing, though grudgingly, to accept costly devices that are intended to scrub the noxious gasses that would otherwise spew out of our automobiles. And we are willing to put up with various regulations intended to control environmental pollution of one kind or another. But we are clearly unwilling to confront the possibility that regulating by-products might not be enough to save our environment from ruin. We might indeed have to cut back drastically our industrial capacity. We might have to do without innumerable conveniences that no home should be without in order to make such a cutback possible. But what do you think the chances of a presidential or congressional candidate running on such a platform today would be?

Granted that not every scientific projection proves to be accurate. Many cries of alarm prove to be false. But when there is a preponderance of evidence that thataway lies doom, what should we do, wait until it is too late? Or bite the bullet and face up to the unpleasant but perhaps lifesaving alternative?

Environmental disaster, of course, isn't the only fate that we seem unwilling to confront. The holocaust of a nuclear war may be much more immediately on our horizon. Yet here too we seem unwilling to make the hard decisions that might obviate that kind of catastrophe. As not only the major powers but minor powers as well continue to multiply and stockpile increasingly horrible weapons of death, the possibility of a cataclysmic war breaking out almost spontaneously increases geometrically. (Who is to say that Idi Amin or a new Reverend Jim Jones will not in the foreseeable future possess hydrogen bombs or cruise missiles?)

Many who have studied this problem carefully are convinced that only by cutting stockpiles of armaments to the bone, with one of the major powers acting unilaterally if necessary, and by totally banning the manufacture of new weapons can we avoid a fiery Armageddon. Yet there is not only little willingness among us to take dramatic steps, it is questionable whether even the pitifully modest SALT agreements can win popular approval from the American people.

It's not that we don't know about the environmental and military disasters that lie ahead on the road we're traveling. We don't want to think about them. Let's pull the blankets over our heads and after a while if we're very quiet, the bogey man will be gone.

Some Humor Is Out of Bounds

IT is, I think, a sign of maturity when a person or a group is able to make themselves the butt of jokes. Jews, for example, have for a long time been able to laugh at their own foibles and peculiarities and I suspect that they developed that cultural ability to laugh at losers during centuries in the ghetto when they could see no light, even at the end of the tunnel.

Catholics, too, have developed an ability to laugh at themselves although we haven't always been as willing to share our putting down of self with the rest of the world as, say, the Jews. In one of Philip Barry's plays, Ethel Barrymore as a nun visiting her family asks, "Is everyone here Catholic?" Being assured that they are, she says, "Good! Now we can talk about the pope."

But there are jokes and jokes. Jews joke about overprotective Jewish mothers, fund raising, and upwardly mobile rabbis. Catholics joke about golf-playing monsignors, fund raising, and overprotective parish housekeepers. But Jews don't joke about the Torah and Catholics don't joke about the Eucharist.

I am moved to make these comments because it seems to have become fashionable in "the best of circles" to repeat cute little phrases and quips that ridicule Catholic religious beliefs. People who wish to seem sophisticated find it amusing when ordering a cocktail to order a "Virgin Mary" (which, for the unsophisticated, is a Bloody Mary without the vodka). Or again, in the square and righteous world of professional football it has become fashionable to mock our devotion to the Immaculate Conception of Mary. A few years ago, a forward pass thrown in a crucial National Football League game bounced off the hands of a defensive back into the hands of the original receiver and became known as "the Immaculate Reception." This year, a controversial play in which one team deliberately fumbled the ball into the end zone became known as "the Immaculate Deception." It was so described by none other than Howard Cosell and a *Sports Illustrated* writer reported that the owner of a team defeated by this play intended to wear "a humorous T-shirt" reading "Immaculate Deception" to the next league meeting.

I find no fault (although others might) with describing a football pass thrown in desperation by the losing team in the waning minutes of the game as "a Hail Mary pass." I'm sure that this phrase was coined by a devout Catholic who had often said a Hail Mary when his own situation was a losing one. But I found the usage of a *Chicago Sun-Times* reporter writing that "from then on, it was Hail Mary, full of haste," thoroughly offensive.

The ease with which these phrases are tossed about and the magnitude of the public forums before which they appear lead me to believe that they have been used unwittingly. But it shouldn't be forgotten that "unwitting" means without wit and implies that the user is not too bright.

At the other end of the spectrum I find the humor of another kind of sophisticate perhaps even more offensive. This is the literate, terribly clever, just a little jaded, don't you know, Catholic or former Catholic who recalls, however unreliably, her or his Catholic childhood. Some of these are amateurs, seeking only to be the life of the cocktail party; others are professional, grinding out longplaying records.

In the 1940s, the talented J. F. Powers in one of his books of fiction told of a nun who solemnly warned the girls in her classroom never to wear (reflecting) patent leather shoes. It was an amusing incident in context but over the years it has become part of Catholic folklore until today there are those who would have us believe that no Catholic girl escaped that advice. And every adult Catholic has at least one humorous or even bizarre confessional experience but there are comedians who want the uninitiated to think that that usually humdrum Saturday experience was a long-running knee-slapper to rival *All In The Family*.

In *Commonweal,* Abigail McCarthy has written: "A good number of former Catholics who gibe, with what they fancy as great good humor, at old practices and beliefs . . . often display a complete and feckless ignorance of the changes in the church and hold that I believe things that I have never believed. They are

forever telling old horror stories about their paro-
chial-school life (that are) so contrary to my experience."

I am surely not suggesting that we Catholics should
go around with chips on our shoulders looking for
someone to knock them off. But I am suggesting that
we blow the whistle on sports commentators who
mock the solemnity of our religion and that we water
the drinks of the Beautiful People who find brittle
humor in apocryphal stories of Catholic experience.

Leave Them Alone and They'll Come Home (Or Will They?)

WHATEVER happened to young people in our churches? I don't mean young people of school age or the young marrieds in their late twenties and early thirties: I mean particularly those whose ages fall in between.

Look around you at Mass next Sunday (discreetly, of course). You will see young people of grade school, high school, and the early years of college age but seldom will you see youthful faces beyond that age. Please understand that I am not basing these comments merely on my personal observations. I know that the topic stated in my first sentence above is one of the most commonly discussed wherever pastors, religious-education directors, and other concerned Catholics gather.

There has traditionally been some attrition in churchgoing among Catholic "twenties" and the conventional wisdom has been not to worry. When they married and began to raise families they would come back, if only "for the sake of the kids." But several things about this view have changed in the last 10 or 15 years. The attrition rate has increased dramatically and many young marrieds have failed to come back.

Grasping at straws, it is possible that this conduct is true of only a single generation and that the pendulum will swing back. But don't count on it. Educators tell us that college students have changed greatly since the 1960s. They are, we are told, far more serious, squarer if you will, than their counterparts in that earlier decade. We are told also that there is a greatly heightened interest in things religious among young people. But only time will tell if this greater seriousness and heightened religious interest will keep them from falling away or bring them back as they grow older. So, I suppose, the question confronting us is: Can those of us who care about the problem do anything to solve it? Two things come to mind, one that applies to all age groups, the other to young people only.

Young people, I believe, must in the first place be made to feel welcome in our churches and in our church activities. The simplest, most straightforward way to make them feel welcome is to involve at least some of them in the various church ministries and activities. Does our parish number young men and women among its lectors, ministers of the Eucharist, ushers? Are young people encouraged to become a part of our parish council? (It might be necessary to reserve a "youth slot" to insure young membership in a parish council.) Are young people included in the planning of the liturgy and whenever lay people are involved in the financial management of the parish? Pastors might be surprised to learn that there are 25-year-old M.B.A.s and 27-year-old attorneys available to help in their parishes.

Robert E. Burns

I realize that the involvement of any lay people in parish life in other than a supernumerary capacity is a relatively new experience for Catholics. Most lay Catholics are accustomed to waiting for a call from on high. Few will take it on themselves to write a letter or knock on the rectory door offering their assistance in the life of the parish. If young Catholics were to do this, the reaction to their volunteering would certainly be mixed. Some would be rebuffed, perhaps even rudely, but others, I'm sure, would be accepted gladly.

Of the parish "jobs" for the young people, those I would most like to see filled would be those with high visibility: lectors, ministers of communion, and ushers. This visibility would be a clear sign to young parishioners that there is a place for them in parish life, that they are indeed welcome in the parish community.

Another subtler but perhaps far more important way in which to make young people feel that they are a welcome part of the parish applies equally to parishioners of all other age groups. The parish liturgy and particularly the homilies must begin where the parishioners are. The homilist, like any good communicator, must ask before beginning, "Do I have reason to believe that my congregation has a built-in interest in my point of departure or will I be in the position of trying to sell electric razors to people not old enough to shave?"

The Examined Life

I have sat and wondered, almost audibly, what young people sitting near me at Mass could possibly find related to their lives when a homilist starts and finishes his remarks in outer space without ever touching the ground. Perhaps it would help if the rest of us got in the habit of praying very fervently for young Catholics and for homilists.

Room with Views for Many

ONE of the insights of the Second Vatican Council—perhaps the most important insight—was the recognition that the church is a community of believers who worship and serve each other. This notion was so strange for most of us that we found it amusing when someone would describe us as members of the people of God. We knew vaguely that the early church, especially the church of the catacombs, was indeed such a community. But we also knew that somewhere along the line the church not only emerged from the catacombs but gradually came to structure itself in a drastically different way. Where the early Christian community had its leaders, chosen from the group, the evolving church of later centuries came to have an appointive, self-perpetuating leadership class. The distinction between chiefs and Indians became clear-cut and inevitably the chiefly class multiplied, spawning big chiefs and little chiefs.

The call of the Vatican Council for the church to return to its original conception broke with the only tradition most of us knew. I recall a typically good-natured column by Father John Reedy at the time. He told how it had taken him years after his ordination to grow relatively secure in his identity as a priest only to find the square outside his window filled with lay people, waving their sweaty nightcaps and shouting, "We are the church!" It was enough to make him wonder if he hadn't got in the wrong line.

But if this seemingly revolutionary conception of the church had impelled some of the serfs to demand their rights and some of the middle-management echelon to gather around the office water cooler to plot for a piece of the action, the average Catholic's idea of the church changed little if at all. To most Catholics then and now the church is still "them" rather than "us." And not only does this mistaken idea sap the vitality of the church, it has even more serious implications.

I know a woman who "left the church" years ago because the priest she had called to bring the sacraments to her dying mother arrived after her mother's death. I know a man who "stopped going" because he believed that the penance assigned him by one confessor was harsh and unfair. We all know people like these who break with the church because of some grievance, just or unjust, against one of "them." Yet it is hard to believe that these defections would have occurred if the nature of the church had been correctly understood. Where is the sense of seceding from a community because one of "us" has done something that turns us off?

Some Catholics, obviously, are turned off for more substantive reasons. Many Catholics seem to have been disillusioned by the promulgated teaching that birth control is always morally wrong. But there is reason to believe that most of those so disillusioned continue to be active members of the Catholic community.

Others have left the Catholic fold for a hundred different reasons. I know intellectuals who claim they can no longer be Catholic because they cannot accept the credibility of Catholic teaching because of birth control or something else. I know also intelligent people, not intellectuals, who have decided they cannot forgive "the church" for changing as it has, for taking away the certainty that old-church morality gave them. At opposite ends of the pole, these people seem convinced that it is only what "they," not "we," do that matters for the church. So they sulk in their tents neglecting an opportunity to be the yeast in the making of a new dough.

Some Catholics—bishops, priests, religious, Catholic teachers, even Catholic writers(!)—tend, of course, to be the more visible members of the community. (I don't know if there's any truth in the rumor that some priests have asked the Missing Persons Bureau to put out an all-points bulletin for their bishop. It's been so long since they've seen him.) Their greater visibility seems to give them a preponderance of importance in the church. But we should not make the mistake of believing that these only speak for the church. Neither should we make the mistake of assuming that the testament of faith reflected from "the others," the faceless masses of Catholics, may not be the most authentic voice with which the community speaks today.

The Examined Life

A community that calls itself Christian and, more important, one that is Christian in its essence ought to have room within it for many kinds of Catholics. It ought, for example, to have room for Archbishop Lefebvre or, even, for me.

Celibacy Is More than a Single Word

CELIBACY, my dictionary tells me, is a religious vow not to marry and it is, of course, the rule for priests and religious in the Roman Catholic Church. As most Catholics know, there are those who believe that celibacy should be, the saying goes, "optional." There should be, they argue, room for both married and celibate clergy in the church.

Those who argue this seem almost invariably to be male and more often than not priests (or former priests) themselves. Curiously, hardly any reformers have taken up the cudgel to argue that celibacy should be optional for religious women and some opinion polls have shown that many who favor the option to marry for priests do not favor the ordination of women to the priesthood. Whether or not this reflects a sexist bias I leave to the recording angel.

Celibacy is a difficult subject, one that is laced with subtleties and nuances and anyone who would discuss it would do well to begin with an act of humility. But there are certain things that need to be said about it.

It is, in the first place, a positive state. If it is understood as a negative thing, merely the absence of marriage, it would be all but meaningless. It is a solemn commitment to a life in which God is the overwhelming priority. It is an intense, special commitment just as, in a different context, a contemplative dedicates his or her life to prayer.

It is a mistake to consider celibacy, despite its difficulty for many, a higher dedication than that embraced by many married people including clergy of other religions. But it is a unique way of giving a deeper attention to a religious vocation.

The words "bachelor" and "spinster," especially the latter, have taken on unflattering connotations in our time but there are, unfortunately, no adequate, nonpejorative synonyms for them. A bachelor is a man who chooses not to marry because he believes that marriage is not for him. A "single man" may be a bachelor or he may be a person who intends to marry eventually.

I bother with these grammatical distinctions because they point up an important fact about celibacy. There are among the celibate clergy (and religious) both bachelors and those who would have married if they had not chosen celibacy. (Just as, ironically, there are "bachelors" in the ranks of married men.)

I am not arguing here whether the maintenance of an exclusively celibate priesthood is best for the church or whether it is not. But I am suggesting that those who do not understand celibacy disqualify themselves from the argument. And, ironically again, some of those who don't seem to understand celibacy are among its most ardent champions. Celi-

Robert E. Burns

bacy, I think, may have suffered most from the advocacy of priests (yes, and bishops) who are weak-kneed in their commitment to it.

It demeans celibacy, for example, to argue in its behalf that more married priests would be required because of the distraction of other responsibilities or that celibacy saves Catholics the cost of maintaining wives and families of priests. Even more, it demeans celibacy to argue that it is merely a discipline and that those who argue against it are disloyal.

Among Catholics who argue *against* celibacy, the characteristic (of their arguments) that I find too often is a kind of arrogance. This arrogance, probably unwitting, argues from an assumption that there is a priestly caste in the church. To put the matter bluntly, they assume that the priesthood is not merely a special state but that it is a better state. Flowing from this assumption, then, is another assumption that the church will be all but mortally wounded if the number of its priests continues to decline. And this viewpoint, one more irony, is often shared by staunch advocates and fierce antagonists of celibacy.

The finger can also be pointed at some of our Protestant and Jewish friends for their patronizing attitude toward Catholics and celibacy. While probably believing that they are being sympathetic, they contribute not at all to ecumenical fellowship when they view celibacy as "quaint" and offer simplistic solutions to the problems it occasions.

The Examined Life

Most Catholics, I assume, wish for an increase in vocations to the priesthood and the religious life and a diminution of the attrition from these states. But our judgment about celibacy ought not to be influenced by the pluses and minuses so involved.

Some opinion polls have indicated that a majority of lay Catholics would accept, perhaps even favor, a married priesthood. ("Forget it, religious women, no one's interested in you!") While I have some reservations about the wording of the questions in some of the polls I've seen, I have no reason to doubt that this may be true. But without an opinion poll I am convinced of this: The vast majority of Catholic laypeople who continue to pray, pay, and for the most part obey are immensely proud of our celibate priests and religious. We are immensely proud that they are dedicated and strong enough to make a commitment that most of us could not make. We try to be charitable toward those who pooh-pooh celibacy but our resentment of their attitudes sometimes breaks through. We try to be patient with those critics of celibacy whose arguments are condescending and with those "defenders" of it who expose their lack of conviction but it isn't easy. Sooner or later, the church may change the rule of celibacy but for the vast majority of the faithful, I am convinced, it has been and is something to celebrate.

Playing Chicken with Righteous Wrath

FROM time to time I wonder if we Americans have lost our capacity for righteous wrath. We have not, God knows, lost our capacity for indignation. Taxpayer revolts abound and, for many, denying civil rights to those honest enough to admit to homosexual orientation has become a new search for the Holy Grail. But indignation and righteous wrath are not the same.

The word "righteous" has taken on connotations that are less than favorable. It has come to imply a certain smugness and perhaps pomposity, but it is a good word that in its biblical-root sense speaks eloquently of virtue. The wrath of Jesus when he drove the money changers from the temple was righteous in its classical sense although many who since have thought of themselves as playing the role *have* been smug and pompous.

The characteristic of righteous wrath that distinguishes it from mere indignation is, I think, its basis in love of neighbor. Our indignation that our expensive automobile tires are being torn to shreds by potholes while the politicians we have elected seem indifferent to the problem is understandable but probably not righteous. Not righteous, at least, unless we can truthfully say that we are as concerned about the tires of our fellow motorists as we are about our own. But if we take time to look around, there are many abuses that ought to invoke our righteous wrath.

This train of thought began in me when I read an article detailing the terrible effects of irresponsible practices in industrial plants on workers. The article carefully documented the devastating and possibly irreversible physical effects on workers forced (work or be fired) to work without precautions of any kind in a plant producing diethylstilbestrol or DES. After exposure to this powerful hormonal substance, the men involved developed feminine characteristics that have continued in some instances even several years after having worked in the plant. One 28-year-old man was forced to undergo a double masectomy which his (former) employer was kind enough to pay for but which has left him scarred, both physically and psychologically.

What may have aroused my wrath in this matter, whether righteous or not others will have to decide, was the penalty the offending industry was assessed. Although government inspectors determined that the neglect of environmental safeguards was clearly willful on the part of the employer, its punishment was a $34,000 fine. And the employer is contesting that! If I cut someone with a knife, I can be sentenced to prison for a felony but if my willful neglect does irreparable damage to dozens of my employees, I can buy my way out with some of the profits that my my-neighbor-be-damned policies have made possible.

Chickens, I learned from the same article, are inclined to peck to death one of their own if it starts to bleed for any reason. Chicken raisers, understandably, don't like to lose a single one of their brood and the answer is vitamin K, a coagulant. But if the workers in a plant producing vitamin K ingest too much of the substance, their own blood begins to congeal with such possible short-term effects as heart attacks and such possible long-term effects as God only knows. (And this is not to mention the possible long-term effects on the blood of people who eat such unpeckable chicken.)

Perhaps the cruelest irony of this particular abuse is the use that is made of vitamin K when it is produced. It is mixed with cattle feed to produced the marbled steaks that in this last third of the 20th century we consider beautiful.

Instances such as those described here, of industries that profit without care for the welfare of their employees or indeed of the general public, can be multiplied many thousands of times. If and when these despoilers are caught, the evil they have done is almost always considered a civil rather than a criminal matter. The manufacturer who dumps tons of pollutants into the public waterways and endangers the health of untold thousands is fined. The person who steals a shrinkwrapped package of pork chops or a pair of panty hose may go to jail.

There seems to be something wrong with our priorities if not with our values themselves. And while "playing God" is a term of opprobrium, it is through us that God works his will. Punishment by rushing waters, crumbling mountains, or burial in molten lava is reserved for Cecil B. DeMille-type epics. Considering our indifference to evil and the infrequency of our righteous wrath, it's just as well.

Butter Will Melt on
Forked Tongues

THE successful effort of the National Rifle Association to flout the will of the majority of Americans is well known. Despite the fact that public-opinion polls repeatedly show that a substantial majority of Americans favor strong gun-control laws, the NRA lobby prevents this wish from being expressed in law by intimidating legislators. Concentrating on one issue, gun control, the skillful (and well-heeled) lobbyists warn legislators that a significant bloc of voters, mobilized by the NRA, will judge them on this one issue only. No matter that a congressman may be a splendid public servant in every other area of legislation. If he votes contrary to the wishes of the gun bloc, its members will vote against him and do everything possible to defeat him when he runs for reelection.

I suppose I shouldn't be surprised that some advocates of ordination of women to the priesthood appear to follow the same one-issue strategy, but I am. A little surprised, at least. I have no problem with the idea of ordaining women and I find the arguments advanced against it unpersuasive. But just as there are, I know, people who sincerely believe that gun-control laws would be harmful, there are many Catholics who honestly believe that it would be wrong to ordain women or at least that the time is not ripe for such change in long-standing practice. But there is no room in the Doomsday Book of the one-issue people for sincere disagreement with them. You buy the whole package or else.

Not too long ago our editors instituted the *U. S. Catholic* Award to be given annually to the person, woman or man, who is judged to have done the most to advance the cause of women in the church. For the first recipient of this award, the judging panel chose Sister Agnes Cunningham, a distinguished teacher and scholar, who was the current president of the Catholic Theological Society and coauthor of the watershed study of human sexuality published that year. But, alas, Sister Cunningham has a fatal flaw: she had earlier expressed less than total support for the ordination of women. "What an outrage!" cried the one-issue people. "How dare you honor someone who doesn't agree with us."

Several of these zealots importuned the editor of our magazine demanding that the award be withdrawn. One gratuitously impugned the motives of Sister Cunningham in opposing their one issue. So intemperate was some of their language that I suggested that our response to their bad-mannered ultimatums be, "We know you are Christians by your love."

On another occasion I was also surprised, but this time pleasantly, when a group that I suspected might have a one-issue mentality proved not to have. I had written some mildly critical comments about Catholic charismatics and knowing the intensity that some of this group bring to their dedication, I expected some hotheaded response. But while a few of the charismatics scolded me for what they considered my lack of insight, all of them did so with charity. It speaks well, I think, for their "movement."

In Nazi Germany, voters were presented with a ballot containing only a single square to be marked, a square placed in front of the word, "Ja." But in a democratic society and in a church that we hope is becoming increasingly democratic there ought to be room for sincere disagreement and there ought to be a realization that there are always many issues to be weighed when judging our neighbor.

Steak Sauce Won't Help Oatmeal

EVANGELIZATION is a word that Catholics have trouble swallowing. Like "ministry," it goes down hard. Yet it's a word we have to use because the word "convert" has been defrocked, so to speak.

Let no tears be shed for the demise of "convert," though. Even though a convert was often an irreligious person, it always had connotations of victory over the enemy. A convert, inevitably, was someone rescued from the enemy camp and pressed into service on our side. Many converts, of course, "came over to our side" as an accomodation to the Catholic party to a mixed marriage. Others became Catholics as part of one intellectual movement or the other. But on encountering a particularly active convert maker, it would not have been unreasonable to look for scalps on his or her belt. So, if we are uncomfortable with the word "evangelization" it is nonetheless a significant improvement.

Most of the energies of evangelizing these days are directed toward the "unchurched" and what a massive target that is. The term is usually applied to those who do not or no longer "belong" to a church but it could be applied as well to those who belong but do not attend regularly. Is there some illumination that can be provided for these, some persuasive argumentation or some edifying witness that will bring these strayed sheep into the fold?

The "in" formula for evangelization is, of course, the use of all the media, especially the electronic variety—radio and television. It would be foolish not to make use of modern methods of communication. The church has always done this. St. Paul was among the first to extend his apostolate beyond face-to-face encounters when he sent his letters, probably entrusted to one of his disciples to deliver orally. When the printing press was invented, religious tracts were produced in abundance and books and periodicals soon followed. Religious programs have been a part of radio and television from their beginnings but until recently they were part of the broadcasting ghetto. Media executives made available to religious groups only the undesirable time slots that paying customers didn't want and in addition they concluded, with considerable accuracy, that religious programs wouldn't be very good.

But in the last five years or so, a new breed of religious cat has found the formula: Develop a classy broadcast package that will grab a sizeable audience, ask their devoted viewers and listeners to send them contributions and, following an upwardly mobile schedule, buy desirable time. So far, so good but what is the value of this kind of evangelizing?

The always perceptive Martin E. Marty, writing in a recent issue of *Context,* confesses to uneasiness about the highly successful "electronic church."

There is, in the first place, a lack of theological substance in the outpourings from these electronic pulpits (a better term, perhaps, than electronic church because there seems to be precious little worshipping involved). The emphasis in these programs seems to be largely if not exclusively inspirational, not a bad thing in itself but a little like Worcestershire sauce without the roast beef. No one, to my knowledge, has surveyed the audience for these programs but it's easy to believe that for many, the electronic church is becoming a substitute for rather than a supplement to a worshipping community of believers.

The electronic church that flourishes today is not really new. Thirty years ago, devotion to the Sorrowful Mother was so popular in Chicago that mounted police had to control traffic at some of the dozens of churches that conducted Sorrowful Mother novena services. The churches were packed but the quantum leap for the devotion took place when a local radio station began to broadcast weekly services. In the comfort of their homes, countless Catholics could respond to a priest leading novenites in the recitation of the Rosary and even join in singing the closing hymn, "Good Night, Sweet Jesus." (The brash young editors of the fledgling magazine, *Today,* expressed their disdain for this cloyingly sentimental hymn in an editorial titled, "Let's Kiss 'Good Night, Sweet Jesus' Goodby.") But the electronic church of today is light years ahead of these modest productions. They are smoothly prepackaged and presented, smacking more of Busby Berkeley than of Bethlehem.

We would be foolish if we did not make use of all the media in our efforts to evangelize. But if we recognize honestly the subtlety and complexity of the Word, we will realize that we cannot present it facilely. The religious commentator who claims to have an answer to all of your religious questions is a faker. And the religious commentator who claims that finding your way religiously is easy is a charlatan. The Holy Spirit writes where he will. He doesn't make command performances.

Mary Most Human,
Pray for Us

"BRING Flowers of the Fairest," are the first words of a hymn sung for many years, and I suspect still sung in many places, during the crowning in May of a statue of Mary. One of the findings of our *U.S. Catholic* survey of parishes is that 59 percent of the parishes continue to observe the May crowning, presumably with the traditional wreath of flowers.

Subjected to critical analysis, "Bring Flowers of the Fairest" is a sugary, perhaps even bathetic hymn. But I am convinced that not only does it evoke happy associations for many Catholics, more than that it recalls to them the roots of their devotion to the Virgin Mary.

Devotion to Mary, we know, has suffered many outrages, not at the hands of infidels, but at the hands of those who would make her a goddess, a sorcerer, a plastic amulet on an unreachable pedestal, or even a precinct captain who can get you things that no one else on the block has.

I suppose it was inevitable that Mary would become many things to many people because we really know so little about her. There is little that we can know for sure about her from the Bible. It tells of the annunciation to her that she is to be the mother of God, of her visit to her cousin, Elizabeth, the nativity story, her ritual purification, and her part in the incident of Jesus in the Temple. None of the evangelists who wrote of these events were witness to them and after the public life of Jesus began we hear of Mary only in connection with the marriage feast of Cana and at the crucifixion. With the possible exception of her role at the marriage feast (and what crimes have been committed in interpreting this story—was Mary really no more than a Jewish mother substituting wine for chicken soup?), we learn little from these stories about Mary as a person.

In the years since, the church, understandably, has felt the need to define theologically and, less understandably, humanly, the kind of person Mary was. Church fathers debated for centuries before deciding in the 19th century to declare that Mary was free from sin from the moment she was conceived in her mother's womb. St. Bernard of Clairvaux, deeply devoted to Mary, opposed the definition as doctrine of the Immaculate Conception. The declaration of the doctrine of the Assumption into heaven took longer—until the 20th century—but even here there was much dispute among the fathers of the church. Theologians in the East, for example, embraced this doctrine with the understanding that it meant that Mary went to sleep at the moment of her "death" and her body remained ever incorruptible. This interpretation continues to be taught in the eastern churches and many the school child who would find this understanding of the doctrine easier to comprehend than the version we learned in the West.

Since Vatican II the tendency in the church has

been to define Mary in less godly and more human terms. We rarely hear her described as mediatrix or co-redemptrix. The council statement on Mary was a carefully worded compromise, arrived at after tortuous "bargaining" among holders of differing opinions but its effect has been to encourage the projection of Mary's humanity from closer studies of biblical texts.

A case can be made, and Patricia Noone does so in her fascinating book, *Mary for Today,* that our understanding of Mary has been deficient and even skewed because the "jury" that has evaluated and defined her has been exclusively male. For some of us, for example, Mary is preemptively the Blessed Mother because isn't motherhood what women are all about? It may never have occurred to us that Mary was a woman apart from her motherhood, living the circumscribed role of a Jewish woman in the first century but a woman nonetheless who loved, became angry, impatient, frustrated, and depressed as well as overjoyed.

Although Christians other than Catholics are devoted to Mary, devotion to her is, I think, especially a mark of a Catholic. I have no proof of this and I'm not sure of its significance but I guess that no person with a strong devotion to Mary has ever drifted away from the church.

Please God, may our growing understanding of Mary as a person, a woman, make this mark of faithfulness ever more true in the years ahead.

A Parish Needn't Be
a Precinct

DURING my college years I spent a lot of my time working in gas stations. While I was on duty at one of these one afternoon, a car pulled up to the island where the driver, a man with an unmistakably Irish face, observed me for a moment, then asked: "And what parish are you from?"

Some years later a Catholic who had been raised in New York surprised me by saying that until he came to Chicago he hadn't heard Catholics identifying themselves and others by the parish "they were from." But as readers of Edwin O'Connor's fine novels know, this is the custom elsewhere, in Boston at least. And as the Irish in their native land identify by the county of the family's origin, many generations of American Catholics are known by their parish. I guess that a person's place of employment is replacing parish as a means of establishing identity for younger Catholics but for many of us, it's still, "She's from Our Lady of Grace," or "He's from Isaac Jogues."

I'm not sure whether the entrenchment of this custom in U.S. Catholic life or the possible passing away of it today has any lasting significance. Its origin may have had something to do with Catholics in embattled enclaves in a predominantly Protestant and presumably hostile environment. But because it persisted into a time when Catholics were more to be feared than fearful, there must be other reasons for it as well.

One of these, I believe, is the practical good sense that the idea of the parish makes. As Father Henry Fehren once explained in an article, a church that strives too strongly for informality may lack the glue to stay together. This is not to say that our present parish structuring is a necessity or even the most desirable form.

The norm for our present parishes is territoriality. ("All Catholics living in the area bounded by Fairfax Avenue on the east, by Queen of Angels Cemetery on the north, the Conestoga Expressway on the west, and the sanitation canal on the south.") Exceptions to territorial parishes are viewed as necessary evils: "national" parishes in which dwindling remnants of once-European Catholics or growing numbers of Catholics of Hispanic origin can worship in their native language; campus chapels intended for resident students where outsiders are not turned away but are usually frowned upon; here and there, a parish that worships in a shopping center or a theater; and, few and far between, an informal "faith community" or floating parish.

But while I am convinced that the territorial parish will continue to be the rule in the church for as far into the future as we can see, it need not be the norm. I am arguing strongly for the continuation of parishes but with a new and vigorous emphasis on the flexible parish. Let's, for example, welcome the establishment of ethnic parishes, as extraterritorial as the old national parishes, but bringing people together because they have a mutuality of cultural interests and customs. Existing parish buildings, some perhaps all but abandoned, could be used for such parishes and I am not for a minute suggesting a ghettoized parish. Membership would be completely voluntary and people of Hispanic origin, for example, who preferred the "Anglo-orientation" of their neighborhood parish could choose to belong to it just as white Catholics, who might find themselves more at home with the creativity of a largely black parish, could join there.

Or, again, college-campus parishes would be encouraged to invite young people (and others) to join their community where they might be more likely to find a mutuality of concerns.

Chaplains now celebrate Mass and administer some sacraments in hospitals and in homes for the elderly. Where there is enough interest, why not encourage the formation of actual parishes for older people centering in the worship and sacramental life of a home for the elderly? In some instances, wouldn't it be desirable for the children and relatives of long-term residents of these homes to belong to such a parish and share with their resident relatives the fullness of a true community?

Other types of flexible parishes would suggest themselves, I am sure, once a policy that welcomed and encouraged them was proclaimed. Some, of course, would argue against this idea on the grounds of administrative complexity or, more pungently, on the grounds that they would drain financial support from existing parishes. But in the last quarter of the 20th century, more than a decade after the Second Vatican Council, neither of these arguments will stand scrutiny.

The Council all but mandated administrative decentralization, preferring the risk of occasional deviation to creeping ossification because of rigidity. And a parish that is unable or unwilling to support itself voluntarily ought to be called into question in any event. Is it needed? The days when there was a surplus of priests have passed, probably gone forever. Our plight is nothing like that of the church in the Third World but there is enough similarity to require the examination of every structure, practice, or tradition.

So let's hear it for the flexible parish. The impetus for it may be born of necessity but the development of it might contribute to a flowering of American Catholicism.

Yellow Ribbons for
Red-Blooded Catholics

"TWENTY years ago, a Catholic in a restaurant on Friday was visible: if he was working at his religion, he was eating fishcakes . . . or Lobster Newburg. Twenty years ago, the same Catholic at a New Year's party was visible: he stopped eating—and drinking—at midnight."

Writing in *The Catholic Register* of Toronto, Father Drake Will began a provocative column with these words and pointed out that this visible Catholic "may not have liked it much, but he did it, partly because he was supposed to, and partly because it gave him identity, a flag to wave, a trumpet to blow. . . . Even the chap on his way back from prison wrote to his lady to 'tie a yellow ribbon round the old oak tree.' "

When some, perhaps many, Catholics complained at the disappearance of the Friday abstinence law and the Communion fast, there was a tendency to dismiss their complaints as trivial, as the crabby whines of people who would rather be struck in the mud. But in retrospect there may have been more to their reluctance than that.

This is not to say that the disappearance of these regulations wasn't a step forward. The plight of faithful Mass attenders remaining in their pews at Communion time because they had broken the fast was certainly unnecessary and easily remedied. And the silliness of Catholics sacrificing by substituting Lobster Newburg for hamburger is obvious. But the disappearance of these Catholic "flags" points up the need to find other "yellow ribbons" if the essential attribute of Catholics as a sign of contradiction in our society is to be realized.

There can be little doubt that the earliest Christian communities were signs of contradiction. We have only to look at the large number of martyrs they produced. Their very presence angered and threatened the prevailing way of life. Which leads us to ask the question, is any American Catholic in danger of martyrdom because he or she is so threateningly a sign of contradiction? Perhaps in the 1960s when some Catholics stood side by side with the soon-to-be-martyred Martin Luther King, but it would be hard to think of anyone who so qualified today.

Martyrdom, obviously, is extreme. Is there some other yellow ribbon that 50 million American Catholics might wear that would make them recognizable as signs of contradiction? There are many such and Father Will suggests a few. "The first," he says, "is Sunday. When someone wants to walk no longer with us, he walks away from Mass; when he wants to return, he returns to Sunday Mass."

The second, he says, is "faithfulness to spouse" and adds, "This implies no judgment of the deserted or single spouse, who is as dedicated to faithfulness as anyone, and who shows it in the third sign" which is "children, not the having of them, but being faithful to them." Father Will sees the latter as meaning care and warmth that doesn't consign the welfare of children to public bodies.

Despite Father Will's apparent assumption that there is no "legitimate" vocation to the single life (other, presumably, than a vow of celibacy), his examples, I think, are well chosen although by no means exhaustive.

While much less public, for example, Catholics who refuse to cut ethical corners in their business, professional, or political transactions are surely offering themselves as signs of contradiction in a society where money is almost a god. Suppose it were possible, statistically, to prove that the number of Catholics who cheat on their income-tax returns or fix traffic tickets was far less than our proportion of the U.S. population. Wouldn't that be a yellow ribbon we could wear proudly? But who believes that?

Or again, wouldn't we have reason for pride if we could prove that we demonstrated our concern for the poor and the derelict *even as well as* the Salvation Army?

Our willingness to serve as a sign of contradiction need not be confined to standing in opposition to the immoral and illegal. It can almost be demonstrated in standing apart from morally neutral but distorted values. If the Citizen of the Year is being honored solely or largely because he has piled up wealth (or even inherited a great quantity!) or because she has the highest Nielsen rating on television, is it too much to ask that our bishops or others labeled Catholic, recall a previous engagement that will prevent their attending? (Confessions, of course, have dwindled in numbers but there are always married couples to be counseled.)

It would be splendid if true that you could "know that they're Christians by their love."

If You Haven't Got
a Penny . . .

ALMSGIVING has always been of the essence of religious practice. More than a few heavy-handed jokes, in fact, have as their point the identification of churchgoers by their willingness to pay as well as pray. The church, they would lead us to believe, is one, holy, catholic, apostolic, and collecting.

Despite these jibes, donations should be close to the center of the practice of our religion. There are probably those who can fill their religious needs by walking in the woods or through the meadows and communing with God and/or nature but most of us need a community of believers to remind us that religion requires us to love our neighbors as well as God. And even if our community convenes in a public park or in the southwest corner of the local commuter depot, there's bound to be some expense.

It's obvious, too, from ingesting the history of religion that churchgoers have a healthy track record of giving. For years, travelers in Europe have noted the abundance of cathedrals and other great churches. Even in some of the smallest villages, grand church buildings dominate the modest homes of people whose ancestors, apparently, gave till it hurt in order that these churches be built. Now, also, we are beginning to observe this phenomenon in our American cities. As new generations leave the urban area for the suburbs, substantial, sometimes even enormous, churches are all but abandoned. And once again we are reminded of the generosity of the churchgoing public.

As these churches are reduced to being little more than monuments (many of the European buildings are elegant, their American counterparts are more likely to be quaint or "historical"), it has become fashionable to criticize "the way money was spent on them." But I suggest that we shouldn't be too quick to join this critical chorus. I suspect that the hardworking people whose francs, marks, shillings, lire, and pennies made these churches possible were proud of them, that they didn't begrudge imparting some of the fruits of their labors to an edifice that thrilled them on great feast days.

In the United States, at least as large a share of contributed offerings has gone to support the parochial school system and, always allowing for exceptions, I believe that this money was given gladly. Although it has been tried, tithing has never caught on among Catholics as it has among some Protestant denominations. But, historically, American churchgoers, Catholic as well as Protestant, have given freely and generously, sometimes more than according to their means.

Recently, however, there has been something of a change in the giving philosophy and practice of American churchgoers. Without any documentation to back my hunch, I assume that most churchgoers continue to give spontaneously and with a fair degree of generosity. But I suspect that to an increasing extent, large numbers are approaching almsgiving including religious almsgiving almost as if it were a commercial transaction. Where is the *quid pro quo,* they ask, and for some the only Latin left in their Sunday liturgy is *caveat emptor.*

As a philosophy of giving, this isn't a bad attitude. An increasingly better educated membership knows that all contributed money is not used wisely or even, in a few cases, honestly. Widely publicized instances of contributed funds being mismanaged or engorging treasuries unnecessarily have made many skeptical. Donors surely have a right to know how the money they give is being used.

But in practice, the hard-nosed attitude, so legitimate in theory, often becomes a habit of contributing little or nothing because what I give might be misused.

On a recent Christmas morning I was drafted to pass the basket at one of the Masses and I was astonished at the number of parishioners who ignored the basket completely and by the meagerness of many other offerings. This on Christmas day, in a predominantly middle-class parish in an era when it's possible to leave a supermarket poorer by $10 or $12 with only a small bag of groceries to show for it. Some of those who stiffed the part-time usher that morning undoubtedly had the best of reasons. A Christmas Eve trip through Toys-R-Us or K Mart might have reduced them to temporary destitution. But all of them?

My point, nevertheless, is not that Americans are giving less generously to religion. The statistics show otherwise. Giving to religious causes has increased year by year without fail (although increases in recent years have failed to keep pace with inflation). My concern, I think, is with the gradual erosion of spontaneity in giving. I notice it in myself as I pass the Salvation Army kettles, frequently telling myself that I will send them a check that will more than aggregate the offerings I would drop.

Perhaps this is inevitable. The futurists tell us that we are approaching a cashless economy. A few churches and some charities encourage their contributors to give by credit card and we already have the capability to transfer funds from a donor's bank account to that of a church or charity. But I think we will have lost something.

It's obviously unwise to send currency through the mails but many people who wouldn't spend a penny without receiving the merchandise purchased or a receipt in the form of a cancelled check continue to make religious donations in that manner. Unwise it is but I think the practice continues to flourish because the donors are giving to God's work and let those who would divert the offering from its intended purpose answer for their own iniquity.

Consistent Respect for Life

ANNUALLY we celebrate Respect for Life Sunday in our churches. Fervent, sometimes even emotional, homilies are preached calling upon Catholics to unite in combating the twin evils of abortion and euthanasia. In some places, Catholics who were unwilling to join this fight were invited to "leave the church."

Let me say at the outset that I am as opposed to the killing of the unborn and the aged as any of these homilists. I think that the overemotional arguments used by some of those crusading against abortion are both unnecessary and likely to turn some in the opposite direction but that is not basic to the issue. I also believe that, as with all moral questions, the specific, practical remedies to be advocated are matters open to differing opinions. Equal rights for women is, I think, a moral imperative but a Catholic (or any moral person) is perfectly free to espouse or oppose the ERA amendment. In the same way, people united in opposition to abortion should be free to favor or disapprove a constitutional amendment forbidding abortion. That is a practical, political if you will, matter rather than a moral one.

But having reiterated my opposition to abortion and euthanasia, I think I have a right to insist on a package deal. I insist that those who claim to respect life demonstrate their concern for human life consistently, not just in areas of their choosing. I don't intend to argue here against capital punishment or war although I do believe that there is an equation between this concern and the concern of the Respect for Life movement. Neither am I unaware that those engaged in this movement argue with reason that a movement has only so much energy and that it must be focused sharply to gain the maximum effect. I am also willing to assume that concern for human life in other forms may be present in meetings and conclaves of the Respect for Life people. It's just that I'm looking for evidence of it.

Where, for example, is there evidence of concern among Catholics (not just those active in the Right to Life movement) for the elderly people who live in rat- and roach-infested tenements such as those in Chicago's Uptown district? How much concern is there that many of these people never leave their miserable lodgings (and they must live there because that's all they can afford) because they fear, with reason, that they might be mugged? Does anyone other than a few dedicated but hopelessly overextended good Samaritans care that some of these "prisoners" cannot even get out of their chairs to feed themselves or use the bathroom unless a kindly volunteer stops by to help them? And what of the elderly, blind lady described by one volunteer who was unaware that the meager lunch she was eating was overrun with cockroaches? May I add that anyone who thinks these instances are rare is living in a fool's paradise.

Robert E. Burns

I would like to see some widespread concern for the human lives that are rotting under incredible conditions in our scandalous prisons. There is in Rome a small building near the Forum that contains the room in which Saints Peter and Paul are believed to have been imprisoned. As small, dark and primitive as it is, it is a merciful place of incarceration compared to some of the cages in which we confine men and women nearly 2000 years later. And please keep in mind that the vast majority of people in American prisons are guilty of one crime only: they are poor. Anyone who cares enough to look will find that people of even average income in our prisons are very, very few. Where then is our concern for these people whom we sweep under the rug so as not to be embarrassed by their presence?

I would like to see widespread concern for the lives of young people who stand on countless corners of our cities because there are no jobs for them and nobody gives a damn. If we do not demonstrate Christian concern for the plight of these young people, we ought at least to act from practical motives because they constitute a gigantic time bomb that will inevitably explode with incalculable cost if we do not remedy the situation.

I sincerely respect the Christianity and good faith of the Respect for Life people. I ask only that they ask themselves, individually and in their meetings, if they are as concerned about human life wherever it exists as they are about the life of the unborn. If the answer is·"yes," I will be reassured. I do not ask that they divide their efforts to help those such as I have mentioned here. I pray only that they and all other moral people will sensitize their consciences to respect all human life.

Affirmative Action and the Prodigal Son

PUT yourself, if you will, in the place of a parent who has just adopted or taken in as a foster child a small girl or boy who has been severely neglected. Perhaps he has been physically abused or perhaps she has been malnourished or left alone in a frightening atmosphere. In any event, the child has been deprived of the love and affection that even irrational animals need to grow and ultimately to survive.

You would, I am sure, make every effort to make up for the love and attention that this child had been denied. You would know that it was not enough to treat this child the same as a child who had not been so deprived. Just as it is necessary to feed a person who is recovering from a wasting illness an extraordinary diet to build him or her back to normal, you would try to give the child an extraordinary emotional diet.

The younger brother of the New Testament's prodigal son didn't understand this. He couldn't or wouldn't accept the fact that his brother, who had squandered his inheritance, badly needed the extravagent love that his father showered on him when he finally returned. For whatever reason (the New Testament writer doesn't tell us why) the wastrel son had greater need for the love and affection of his father.

The Examined Life

Our pragmatic society has little patience with such a concept but it is, I think, of the essence of Christianity. We exalt equality but our idea of equality sometimes comes down to this: A hungry person and a well-fed person encounter a loaf of bread simultaneously. Too often we consider equality to be a half a loaf for each. But if the well-fed person is a Christian, wouldn't he or she tell the hungry one, "It's yours"?

In an attempt to make up the neglect and deprivation that various minorities have suffered, we have in this country instituted programs called affirmative action programs. Businesses and schools particularly have agreed to accept, in the case of schools, and to employ and promote, in the case of businesses, qualified members of minorities in preference to members of the majority. Sometimes the minorities are racial or religious; sometimes they are women. (There are more women than men in the United States but far fewer in the work force.) Some affirmative action programs are voluntary, even spontaneous, but more often than not they are in response, direct or indirect, to laws or governmental fiat.

Not everyone, of course, is enthusiastic about affirmative action programs. Like the younger brother of the prodigal son, some feel that dividing the loaf of bread equally (read justly) must mean dividing it half and half. But the malnourishment produced by many years of deprivation is there to be seen, and without a compensatory program such as affirmative action this long neglect would not be overcome in several lifetimes.

In some places and situations an attempt is made to go one step beyond affirmative action by establishing "quotas," a predetermined number of members of each minority to bring a kind of balance to a grouping. Unlike affirmative action programs, quotas usually waive the requirement of equal qualification that affirmative action programs have. (I believe that quotas are sometimes justified but I am not arguing that here.)

I am not, I assure you, going to tell you that if Jesus were living in the United States today, he would favor affirmative action programs. I am not even going to search for an exemplary saint who instituted similar programs in her apostolate. This is a problem that we will have to work out for ourselves. But I don't see how anyone could consider a program Christian that would do less than affirmative action programs try to do.

Watergate, Watergate . . . Everywhere

WHAT have we done wrong? As a matter of fact, what are we doing wrong even now? Here we are, a nation that not only prides itself on being God-fearing but also on what may be the most highly organized system of religious education in history. (This is true of Protestants, Catholics, and Jews alike.) Yet we are, I believe, as immoral a people as any that have preceded us.

Perhaps we should stop here for a brief word-association test. When I say "immoral," what word comes first to your mind? If your answer is "sex" or a spinoff of that popular term, please turn and face the blackboard. Morality has to mean much, much more than that or it means nothing at all. Further, if sexual morality were our only concern today, our American society would fare pretty well when compared with other societies. For all the talk about the new sexual freedom, historians know that many other societies were far more libertarian (if less talkative about it) than ours.

But I find it hard to believe that any society could have been less honest than ours is. From the wealthiest to the poorest, from gigantic publicly owned corporations to individuals acting almost alone, we must be the most eminently purchasable people ever. If it isn't true that everyone and everything has its price (and, of course, it isn't), the exceptions are not numerous.

Item: In full view of visitors to a large city courthouse, shabbily dressed recipients of traffic violation tickets can be seen almost any day of the week paying petty officials to wipe out the "case" against them.

Item: Numerous U.S. congressmen admit that they have taken money from a shadowy Korean lobbyist. Their defense is that they didn't do anything in return for these payments, but surely they were aware that this man from another country wasn't solely interested in promoting good government when he "contributed to their campaigns." Two ironic footnotes to these disgraceful transactions were the elaborate procedures used to "launder" the gifts in some instances and the lowness of the price that some congressmen set for themselves.

Item: The two chief manufacturers of a pesticide recently found to cause sterility in chemical workers knew more than 20 years ago that the same pesticide caused sterility in amimals. Results of tests of this pesticide by Dow and Shell Chemical companies (I want to be sure that these companies get the credit) were published in a scientific journal in 1961, but neither the chemical workers nor the federal agency charged with protecting them knew about the tests until 38 male workers were found sterile.

In asking myself, "where did we go wrong?", I tried to recall what I was taught about honesty in the many years of religion classes I attended. I confess

The Examined Life

that my clearest memory was of the distinction between lies and white lies. A white lie, I recall, was one that employed mental reservation. It was all right to tell a vendor at the door that my mother wasn't home when she was because I was really saying, "My mother isn't home (to you)." For all I can recall, I may have received sound catechesis regarding honesty but for some reason, only the white lie escape clause sticks in my memory. I wonder why. And is it possible that such a trivial aspect of an important virtue took vivid shape in the memories of many besides me and became a leak in the dike through which torrents of dishonesty poured? It seems preposterous and yet does anyone have a better explanation?

There is, to be sure, the tried and true explanation provided by the historic colonizing process in America. The frontier spirit, we have been told, accounted for a lot of things that are distinctive in the American character. Could it be that as a people we became accustomed to taking what we pleased from the Indians and from the unspoiled, virginal environment? Only the superior strength or the superior guile or the superior persistence of an enemy or a rival inhibited the acquisition of what we wanted. And if one of these was sucker enough to sell us Manhattan Island for a beaded $24, only in America!

The massive dishonesty of Watergate seemed to occasion a healthy revulsion among the American people. This could be construed as a ringing vote for honesty but I wonder to what extent it really was. I

Robert E. Burns

am convinced that the investigation of the Watergate scandal would never have got off the ground except for the oafishness of its perpetrators and, more important, because many of the overwhelming majority who had voted for the principal villain felt betrayed and personally suckered by the turn of events.

All of which, nevertheless, leaves us with our unexplained failure to educate for honesty. We could, I suppose, cop out by saying that school children learn dishonesty at home and, I am sure, there is truth in this. But shouldn't we be able to overcome this?

I regret that I am unable to offer a suitable prize for the reader who provides the most creative explanation for or, better yet, solution to this problem. But I will be grateful and I promise to think fondly of her or him far into the future. Honest, I will.

Save Our Syntax

SOMEDAY, I hope a well-qualified social scientist with the necessary time and money will explore the correlation between the way people speak and the way that they act. During the explosive '60s, for example, the sour-tempered but perceptive poet, Karl Shapiro, concluded that the young people who were then rebelling in a variety of asocial ways were acting that way because they were fundamentally inarticulate. And anyone who has observed the frustration of a bright child not yet able to speak will appreciate Shapiro's theory.

But, God knows, we're not an inarticulate people today, not if the quantity of speech and other verbal messages is any measure. From waking to sleeping we are bombarded with words and if the illiteracy rate in history's most technologically advanced society is a disgrace, this fact hasn't done much to inhibit the verbal torrents that threaten to inundate us.

The quality of our language is something else again. There is in the first place the multiplicity of jargon. Every subculture—business, sports, science, show business, even religion—contributes to this overabundance. But the very speed with which our media of instant communication broadcast jargon can be a blessing as well as a blight. It is true that rapid communication intrudes this specialized language into our daily lives but this very rapidity causes these alien phrases to become overused, then stale, then forgotten. Some jargon, of course, is hardy. A term like "input" will probably be with us for a while and "feedback" may be a permanent addition to our language but words like "ballpark" (meaning in the vicinity) and "parameters" will, it is to be hoped, fade into oblivion before long.

Rapid communication also is responsible for ushering slang into our lives and just as rapidly showing it the door. For a few years in the 1960s everyone seemed to be "doing his (or her or their) own thing." A person who used that phrase today would be considered quaint (or someone who had been dodging imaginary Japanese on a forgotten Pacific atoll for the past few decades).

Perhaps the most corrosive barnacles to attach themselves to our speech and writing patterns are the pseudo-genteel words, words that catch on because they are thought to give a little more class to our expression. We've always had these—an aunt of mine used to describe someone who played tennis as "toney"—but they had a limited circulation. But today let one public official or talk show host or columnist say "ongoing" when "continuing" is meant and the silly word afflicts us to an epidemic extent. (The former editor of *The Wall Street Journal* once wrote a memo to his staff, to wit: "If I find one more 'ongoing' in the paper I'm going to be downcoming to the newsroom and somebody's going to be out-going.")

Just as pervasive is the use of the pseudo-genteel terms, "hopefully" and "more importantly." A weak but probably valid case can be made for the use of the latter term. It is, of course, technically correct to say, "More importantly, smoking tobacco can lead to cancer as well as stunting your growth," but I doubt that you would find this usage in anything written more than ten years ago. This is because "more important" (short for "what is more important") is quite enough. The extra "ly" is as super-fluous as paper cuffs on lamb chops.

"Hopefully," on the other hand, is an abomina-tion. It has a legitimate if awkward use as when I say, "The swimmer approached the starting block hope-fully." But more often than not the word as used to-day modifies nothing: "Hopefully, the traffic will thin out soon" or "Hopefully, the children will be home soon." Hopeful traffic? And who's hopeful, the children or their parents?

Another pseudo-genteelism is the useless addition of the word "would" before a verb. This is so com-mon today that the correct usage seems almost an ex-ception. "I would think that the President favors this bill." (What's wrong with "I think that the President favors this bill?") Listen for this foolish use of the subjunctive or perhaps I should say don't listen for it. You'll hear it so often that it will drive you crazy.

Robert E. Burns

It may strike you as nit-picking that I deplore this bastardization of the language but I don't think it is. Speaking and writing badly obviously isn't an evil to be equated with the nuclear arms race or hunger in the world but it may well be symptomatic of an "anything goes" mentality that can hardly be anything but debilitating in the long run. As Evelyn Waugh might have said, if he had thought of it: "If the British hadn't stopped dressing for dinner in the tropics, the Empire might never have been lost."

The Importance of the Parish School

IN the last few decades there has been something of a tendency to look down our noses at parochial schools. It has become fashionable in some Catholic circles to declaim that schools "of our own" have outlived their usefulness, that what might have been a necessity for an immigrant church struggling to find its identity has become a luxury in our modern, pluralistic society.

And then there are the economic and "person-power" factors. Some parishes decided that they couldn't afford their own schools, good or not, and others, bereft in a short period of time of their teaching sisters, decided that maintaining schools staffed largely or exclusively by lay people wasn't worth the alarmingly accelerated cost.

But two things seem to have happened to American parochial schools on their way to oblivion. The first of these was the stubbornness or, if you will, determination of many pastors and/or parishioners who flatly refused to abandon their schools. For some, this stubbornness may have been little more than inertia or traditionalism. "We've always had our own parochial school and it would be unthinkable not to have one." But for many this determination was more thoughtfully motivated (about which more later).

Robert E. Burns

The second thing that happened was Father Andrew Greeley. The prodigiously energetic sociologist who raises embarrassing questions and hackles in equal proportion has become the leading and most persuasive advocate of the Catholic school system.

Again and again, Father Greeley's research has demonstrated that the "products" of a Catholic education tend to be better Catholics. When his studies first indicated that Catholic school graduates, as a rule, were likely to be more faithful in attending Mass, participating in the sacraments, and observing Catholic moral teaching, both personal and social, they were seen by some as being against the grain. Hadn't Mary McCarthy and a host of fallen-aways "proved" that a Catholic education was more likely to sour than to nourish? Wasn't it those who were less exposed to Catholic education—the converts and latecomers— who were more likely to keep the faith? But Greeley's research was objective proof, not off the top of someone's head. And what's more, no one arose to offer the results of research that proved the contrary.

More recently Father Greeley's research has shown that American Catholics would be willing to contribute considerably more than at present if they were convinced that this greater sacrifice was necessary to maintain present schools and to build schools in newer parishes. He feels strongly that in the latter, usually suburban parishes, we have given up too easily and have concluded, erroneously, that parishioners would be unwilling to pay the freight involved in building and maintaining schools.

I think that the recent history of the Catholic Church in the United States has proved Father Greeley right. The church in this country has not, traditionally, been a church of the universities and intellectuals as it has been in Europe (although it may be in the future). Neither has it been a church of sociopolitical preoccupations as it is becoming in Latin America and in some other parts of the Third World. American Catholics have been predominantly middle class and if the religious practice of American Catholics has had a unique characteristic, it is this: The men go to church regularly.

I think that American Catholic men practice their religion faithfully because American Catholic religion has traditionally centered around the church *and* the parish school. Catholic couples with young children attend Mass together (the children will soon be ready for parochial school or religion classes). The religious ceremonies centered in the parish school (Holy Week and May processions, graduations in the church, Lenten and Forty Hours devotions) as well as ceremonies involving all the children (First Communion, Confirmation) kept all the family, including fathers, close to the church. And if in recent years, Catholics of post-high-school or post-college age have drifted away from the church, who can say that those who marry and have children of their own won't return when their children get old enough "to notice." Or, to put it another way, how much chance is there that these "driftaways" will return if the schools aren't there to attract them through their children?

Parochial schools, it seems to me, are indispensable for the American Catholic church. If we allow our parochial schools to go down the drain, if indeed we fail to expand our parochial school system, we are asking for trouble.

I am not for a moment suggesting that we ought to accept parochial schools that are inferior scholastically. Neither am I suggesting that parochial schools should be built and maintained at the expense of religious education programs for children attending public schools. On the contrary, I think we must be willing to pay the price to maintain schools in which the quality of teaching (if not the quality of the physical plant) is equal at least to that found in public schools. And I think we should center the religious education program of the parish, for all children and adults as well, in the parish school. If religious education in the parish school is the responsibility of paid professional teachers, it should be available to all who belong to the parish community. (We can't afford to treat public-school students as second-class citizens where religious education is concerned.)

The last 15 years of ferment have, I believe, been awfully good for the church in the United States. It

The Examined Life

has not been without cost but it has been and continues to be healthy. But we can't afford to lose the strengths that have made the Catholic experience here uniquely successful.

Poverty Is OUR Problem

EDITORS of Catholic publications know that there are two important subjects (at least) that their readers are not likely to respond to with any real interest, much less enthusiasm. Their average reader is likely to be turned off if the publication in hand chooses to discuss Latin America or world hunger.

So this is fair warning to those of you who are pale, listless, and depressingly average: Please bug out. I intend to discuss world hunger. I have no fear of losing those of you who are bright, clear-eyed, and decidedly above average. You, I am sure, will stick with me to the finish.

If I needed a hook to hang such a discussion on (I don't really, I'd do it anyway), it would be the agility with which some of those who beat their chests and bellow the loudest that we must unite behind the Pope suceed in ignoring *On the Progress of Peoples.* It isn't sexy, of course, and it doesn't hurl anathemas at those who dare to defy the magisterium. To an extent, it's traditional in the sense that it restates the time-honored concern of the church for the have-nots. But, to a considerable extent, it was (and, ironically, still is) bold and trailblazing. Some of it could even be described as thrilling, a claim not easily made for papal letters.

The Examined Life

Listen to this: "Once more we say: the surplus riches of wealthy countries must help those countries still in need. It is still true, today, to say that charity begins at home. But home, today, is all the world. If help does not arrive, God's judgment and the anger of the poor will both rise up against the rich man's sin of avarice. Civilizations die when they turn in on themselves. The story of the rich man in the Gospel still holds true. God said to him: 'You fool, this night I do require of you your soul.' "

But not only has there been little progress in achieving the goals called for by Pope Paul, it can be argued persuasively that the situation has worsened. At a recent international meeting in Geneva, a sophisticated film presentation produced by Multimedia International, an organization co-sponsored by 35 Catholic congregations, was shown. According to Religious News Service, the 55-minute multivision show, called "One Earth," vividly depicts the problems of the haves, who have too much and use too many of the world's resources, and the have-nots, who are undernourished or even starving. It stresses the point that unless the growing imbalance is short-circuited, the "resulting chaos" may lead to global destruction.

"The recorded commentary, emphasizing that the problem is not insufficiency of food in the world but bad distribution and too much waste, points out that 15,000 people die every day of starvation and that nearly 500 million people suffer from malnutrition while a like number of people suffer from problems connected with overeating.''

At this point, it's logical to ask, what if anything we as individuals can do to right this wrong, to tip the scales in a direction opposite from that in which they are presently weighted. I don't, in the first place, believe that pledging to forego meat on certain days or participating in voluntary Bread for the World campaigns will ever make a whole lot of difference. Not that I don't applaud these efforts for, at least, their witness value. Efforts such as these might even be prerequisite to any more substantial action. But the job of feeding the world's hungry is just too damn big for any voluntary organization or combination of same.

What is required, I believe, is for people who really believe that loving their neighbor is a command of God, to tell their leaders—the President and Congress in the United States—that they are willing to pay more taxes to support energetic government programs to feed, clothe, and shelter those in need, wherever they may live. This, I think, is an obligation of other ''have'' nations—Germany, France, Japan, Canada, for example—as well as our own. But whether these other countries join us or not, our obligation to do far more than we are doing is clear.

If we stop for a moment to consider that the ''have'' nations are spending more than 300 billion dollars every year for armaments alone, how can we

The Examined Life

say that we can't afford to help much, much more. And while I don't have at hand the amounts our countries spend on liquor, tobacco, and other drugs, we all know that the totals are staggering.

I am indebted to one of the voluntary agencies about which I spoke, Food for the Hungry, for this interesting insight:

What was the sin of Sodom, they write. Gross (sexual) immorality? Well, here's something to think about:

"Your sister Sodom's sins were pride and laziness and too much food, while the poor and needy suffered outside her door." (Ezekiel 16:49)

And Pope Paul broadens the challenge to those who remain indifferent in the face of this injustice when he writes:

"Inequality in the sharing of our wealth is not the only scandal crying out for justice. Now, increasingly, the scandal is inequality in the sharing-out of power. In many lands a few rich men still dominate the rest. While they enjoy a civilized existence, the rest stay poor. And worse, they are deprived of any say in how their lives are run. For them both life and work lack human dignity."

Ordaining the Total Woman

THE Vatican Council tried to teach us that "we" are the church. But I don't think this teaching has really caught on. Most Catholic lay people (and even a significant number of priests) continue to think of the church as "they" rather than "we."

This persistent misunderstanding probably can be traced to our early and oft-repeated religious education. We were members of the church, all right. After the publication of a widely-noted letter of Pope Pius XII, we learned that we were members not only of the church but of the Mystical Body of Christ. (That's another elucidation that never really caught on and is rarely heard anymore.) But "we" were rarely invited to exercise our membership other than to do what "they" told us to do. As they might say at IBM, any attempt to input would be counterproductive.

A relative handful of Catholics seem to have taken the teaching that the church is really a community of believers, all believers, differentiated chiefly by the wide variety of roles we are called upon to fill. The perhaps ingenuous insistence of this small band on taking the Vatican Council seriously hasn't been enough to move mountains of inertia but it has had a surprisingly yeasty effect. And in surprising ways.

When enlightened bishops and pastors have offered the nonordained an opportunity to share in a variety of ministries, there were more than enough takers. Lay women and men began to appear on our altars as ministers of the Eucharist and as lectors. Lay men and women, including religious sisters and brothers, were offered expanded opportunities to serve as religious education directors, both professional and volunteer. Parish councils in some places have been given genuine freedom to plan and to some exent direct the activities of the parish community.

But as anyone who has ever worked with yeast knows, it brings about a chain reaction that once begun is almost impossible to stop. Not only do once meek non-participants, now uppity, press increasingly urgent demands for a piece of the action. In increasing numbers they have the effrontery to ask that they be consulted, even (God forbid!) that they be given a kind of vote.

Not surprisingly, this doesn't go down well everywhere. One bishop felt called on recently to proclaim that while all church members other than bishops belong to the "learning church," only bishops comprise the "teaching church." The good bishop's abysmal theology apart, this is an idea whose time is gone. The natives are never going to buy that juju from B'wana again.

I was reminded of all this by the interesting (American) reaction to the recent Vatican statement on the possibility of women being ordained to the priesthood. It was a reaction not all that predictable. A few

Robert E. Burns

bishops hailed it as the greatest Vatican statement since that on sexual ethics but a few other bishops had trouble keeping their indignation out of their statements of loyal acceptance. Some fringe activists among women's groups planned demonstrations in protest but most received the statement with sanguinity. "If this is their best shot," the latter seemed to say, "it's only a matter of time before the battle will be won."

For some of us, a feeling of *deja vu* was evoked by the statement. Visions of Orval Faubus barring the doors of the schools in Little Rock to black children or George Wallace barring the doors to the University of Alabama. And what ever became of them? As I was told as a boy, "Don't say never. Never is a long time."

The crux of the women's ordination problem today, I think, can be found in the comments of a Vatican functionary at the press conference announcing the statement. He presented the results of a survey made by Father Andrew Greeley showing that a majority of the American Catholics surveyed were opposed to the ordination of women priests.

To digress a moment, it's interesting that the Vatican quotes Greeley's findings when they support their conclusions but considers the American sociologist a non-person when his surveys show that an overwhelming majority of American Catholics oppose the Vatican teachings on birth control.

The Examined Life

I believe Father Greeley's conclusion that a majority of American Catholics oppose the ordination of women priests, not only because he is a careful researcher of opinion but also because my own, utterly unscientific, observation leads me to the same conclusion. I think it is beyond question that opposition to the ordination of women is far stronger among women than among men. This is true also of the opposition to the Equal Rights Amendment to the U.S. Constitution. The "total woman" concept is terribly strong among American women. Those who embrace it don't want their roles to change. They cherish the notion that women should be subservient to men and that in return they will be "provided for."

But I predict that the pendulum will swing. Sooner or later, a majority of American Catholic women (and men) will conclude that while the ordination of women is not an essential question, it is one that should be cleared out of the way. They will realize that it will continue to be "in the way" of essential questions as long as a little band of segregationists insist on barring the doors to the admittance of women.

When the pendulum does indeed swing, the discipline of the church will change because the will of the majority will be too strong to resist.

Authority Versus Birth Control

TO begin by stating the obvious, the reason for a law is not negated because many, even most, people fail to observe it. Far more murders are committed today than were committed a generation or two ago (although not so many as a millennium ago) but no sensible person would argue that the increased frequency of murder makes the repeal of laws against it desirable.

The same reasoning applies when the "law" in question is a religious teaching. Backbiting, for example, has been proscribed by the church for centuries but (to rehabilitate a hoary phrase) this law has always been more honored in the breach than in the observance. And despite this the church teaching declaring backbiting a sin is not under attack and it would surprise me if it were in danger of repeal.

But the peculiar history of our "noble experiment" to ban the manufacture and sale of alcoholic beverages in the United States merits consideration when this question is raised. Fourteen years after the so-called Prohibition amendment became law it was indeed repealed. Support for an amendment to repeal it grew over the years for a number of reasons including the realization that the law had spawned organized crime for the first time in American history. But the compelling reason for its rejection was the overwhelming unwillingness of most Americans to accept it as a good and necessary law.

Returning to my comments at the outset, this unwillingness in itself did not gainsay the law, was not "proof" that it should be repealed. But it opened the reasons for the law to serious scrutiny and it placed the wisdom of the law under a powerful microscope.

It should be noted that not only did millions of Americans break the Prohibition law, an even larger number perhaps refused to accept the law as a good thing. Despite the increased frequency of murder in our society, no one that I know of condones murder or advocates the repeal of laws against it. This law, though broken often, is accepted universally.

My ruminations on this subject arise from consideration of the fact that many if not most American Catholics have, incontestably, indicated their unwillingness to accept the church's teaching on birth control. I hope I do not seem to belabor a point (but I do not want what I say to be misconstrued) when I agree that this failure to accept the birth-control teaching is not in itself a conclusive argument against the "law." But it ought to give pause to everyone who loves the church. It ought to make us confront the fact that millions of Catholics who do love the church have drifted away or will drift away from the community because the proscription of birth control under any circumstance makes no sense to them. We ought also to confront the fact that millions of Catholics who have not and may never leave the community continue to dress themselves and their young children in their Sunday best and attend Mass Sunday after Sunday but refrain from receiving the Eucharist because, obviously, birth control has placed them "out of grace."

Most married Catholics refuse to accept the church's proscription of birth control, I believe, because they see its reasoning as based on an understanding of sexuality and even biology that is truncated at best and mythological at worst. The concept that every act of sexual intercourse must be "open to conception" is unreasonable in every sense of the word. In our times, it may be that even without birth control as many acts of sexual intercourse between married couples are not open to conception as those that are. One need only consider the vast number of married couples who are beyond the childbearing age, the wives for whom surgery or other physical conditions have made childbearing impossible and, irony of ironies, the many couples who obediently, doggedly and with endlessly inventive procedures attempt to find the precise time of month in which the female partner is not open to conception.

For many of the couples who continue to stay, then, (and I include those couples, already mentioned, who cling to their pews at communion time) the only "reason" for accepting the teaching against birth control is the argument from authority.

The argument from authority is not to be taken lightly. It alone has kept regiments from panicking under merciless fire from the enemy (as in the Charge of the Light Brigade) and it alone has kept small children from being burned, mutilated or killed by hot stoves, intriguing power mowers, or careening automobiles. But the argument from authority, if it is to be widely accepted by adults and to persevere in time, must be grounded in reasoning that makes sense to ordinary, intelligent, even if non-professional, women and men. People like these, intimately involved as they are in the matter under discussion, are not likely to be impressed by the cool detachment of metaphysical games.

The board of both lay and clerical experts named to advise the Vatican Council was a splendid attempt to bridge the tragic gap between many married couples and many church authorities. But its advice, unfortunately, was pigeonholed. And despite the time sadly wasted since then, another group such as that one might yet lead the way to a generally acceptable solution. Especially if the board has at least as many married as celibate members.

Are Preachers Teachers?

IF Jesus had been content to be just a prophet, life for us might have been simpler (if ultimately less rewarding). But He had to go and found a church and look where that's got us. If He had just said, "Do as I do," his example might have lingered (probably not for long) but He also said, "Do as I say," and the teaching church was born.

One American bishop proclaimed recently that all the faithful except the bishops belong to "the learning church" but that surely isn't what the Second Vatican Council had in mind. That body recognized that "the teaching church" is comprised of a lot of people. Pastors and other priests homilizing at Mass are an important part of it. Theologians delineating in airy bowers or in almost airless apartments, teachers in Catholic schools, dedicated people witnessing among the less religious citizenry and even (heaven forfend!) editors of Catholic publications lighting candles and/or cursing the darkness. The non-professional laity, too, were invited by the Council to bring their unique experience into the service of the teaching church and more than a few wise leaders have welcomed such contributions.

What to teach, of course, concerns all but the most insensitive of those who share the teaching responsibility. The latter shout, "What's wrong with the Ten

Commandments?'' or ''It's just a matter of living by the Sermon on the Mount,'' without giving a moment's thought to the fact that the meaning and implications of these invaluable statements are subject to many interpretations or that they must continually be counterposed against changing cultures and historical circumstances. The agonizing debates about ''pulling the plug'' on Karen Quinlan's life-supporting machines could not have been anticipated even a generation ago. The victims of Roman legionnaires and the victims at Hiroshima were equally dead but the morality of the weapons used must be explored in radically different terms.

Add a dash of separation of church and state and the pot bubbles even more energetically. It's one thing to make the views of the teaching church felt in a nation where a king can't be crowned without the approval of a bishop-primate, an entirely different situation in a country where a president is elected despite the all but expressed opposition of its bishops. But there is no doubt in my mind that the church is far more likely to flourish in the latter, in a democracy such as the United States, provided it ''plays by the rules.''

In the first place, the church in a reasonably free democracy with reasonably free elections must refrain strictly from endorsing candidates, any candidates. Today in Asia and in South America, church leaders, entire hierarchies in some countries, are vigorously opposing national leaders but these are countries in which the citizens are given no choice. A dictatorial government suppresses dissent and forbids real opposition to its regime and the church feels impelled to fight for basic human rights. But in democracies with free elections and other basic freedoms, the church, at all levels, should stay out of the electoral process. As individuals, Catholics, of course, will be involved in the electoral process but "official intervention" is rarely if ever justified in a democracy.

What, then, of attempting to influence legislation, either directly or by influencing others. Is that a function of the teaching church? The answer, I think, is yes, but.

There are church agencies, official bodies, set up to gather specialized information, to disseminate it and on occasion to try specifically to influence legislation or public officials. Almost always, the attempt is based on moral grounds. And it is surely a legitimate function of bishops or of Catholic writers and editors to raise their voices in support of or in opposition to specific legislation. Presently the Catholic bishops believe that a constitutional amendment prohibiting abortion is desirable and in the interest of public morality. Their attempts to have such an amendment passed arise logically from their function as moral teachers in the public domain. They might just as logically push for legislation to prohibit capital punishment or the manufacture and sale of handguns.

The Examined Life

The pulpits of our churches, or rather our altars, are, I believe, another matter. Although I strongly favor the strictest possible gun-control law, I would not want to see that advocated from the altar. Neither would I like to hear legislation outlawing capital punishment, the use of nuclear weapons or abortion advocated during Mass.

The celebrant at Mass is surely an integral part of the teaching church but his role when homilizing about moral issues should be limited to helping the worshippers to arrive at the best possible moral judgment. If he is discussing capital punishment, he should confine himself to discussing the moral issues. The legislative and political judgments belong in another forum.

Strangely enough, we hear all too little discussion of public moral issues (as opposed to matters of private morality) in our churches. I'm pretty sure I wouldn't want to hear editorials from the altar supporting a particular moral judgment, even those with which I agreed (and even when the subject was suggested by the Scripture of the Mass). But I think I would like to hear more (public) moral questions *raised* there.

As I said at the outset, *what* to teach concerns all but the most insensitive. And to that I must add, "and where." Beware of the man or woman with the easy answers.

The Church and the
Single Catholic

AMONG the many interesting letters we receive from
our readers one stands out in my mind. It was an
especially enlightening note from a young man who
had just moved into a parish new to him. He called
the rectory and asked if the parish had any programs
or activities for beyond-teenage single people. The
reply was polite but negative. His parish, like most
Catholic parishes I suspect, had no way, other than
the Mass and the sacraments, for an unmarried parishioner to participate in parish life.

There are obviously various types of "singles" in a
parish in need of various ministries and programs.
The increasing life span of Americans has resulted in
a growing number of widows and widowers. The
striking increase in the number of divorced (and not
remarried) women and men is another sizable segment of the population, a segment until recently all
but ignored by the church. Finally, there are those
who by choice or by circumstance have not married
at all.

The widowed, of course, have a relationship (although it is sometimes a kind of shirttail relationship)
with the parish usually not open to the other two
groups. If a widow doesn't mind being occasionally
"odd-woman-out" or is willing to corral three other
widows to make up a foursome, she can participate

in a parish's womens' club activities. A widower, if he's so inclined, can bowl with the Holy Name men or volunteer to take up the collection.

In some parishes (statistics are not available but I suspect their number is few), doors have begun to open to divorced Catholics. The line that separates divorced and remarried Catholics from the sacramental life of the church still prevails in most parishes but that line doesn't bar the single divorcee. The old admonition to Catholics that they should shun the divorced is rarely if ever heard now, but old warnings are hard to forget and old habits are hard to change. But there is new concern in the church for the divorced and steps, though slow, are being taken to reintegrate the divorced, both the single and the remarried into the life of the church.

The third group of single Catholics is, however, the most neglected. They are almost non-persons except in the perhaps subconscious but nevertheless condescending sense that they are "ladies and gentlemen in waiting." Sooner or later, this attitude seems to imply, they will come to their senses or get lucky and get married. Then and only then will they really belong to the parish, and indeed, to the church.

This attitude, aside from being, perhaps, boorish, is radically unenlightened. It fails to realize that there is and has always been a vocation to the single life. When I speak of a vocation to the single life, I make no reference to sexual orientation. I speak of the way that persons address themselves to "the business of life.'' Sexual orientation is of no concern here because there are celibates (as they should be) who are not cut out for the single life and single people (as they should be) who are not cut out for celibacy.

It is, I suppose, a digression to point out that some priests have found grief when they rushed into marriage when it was their unsuitability to the single life rather than celibacy that drove them to a career change. (Some, for example, might have found far more satisfaction as a part of an extended family.) In like manner, some lay people, despite being ill suited to celibacy, lock themselves into "a celibate existence" because they understand that only in a vocation to the single life can they realize their life work and life goals.

On second thought the example above may not be a digression because the concept of a vocation to the single life, apart from sexual orientation, may have important implications in the matter of vocations to the priesthood and religious life. The celibacy question has loomed so large in recent years that a candidate for a religious vocation, once he has satisfied himself and his religious superiors that he can live with celibacy, is unlikely to be asked if he can live with a vocation to the single life (or more positively, if he prefers a vocation to the single life). The community life of religious priests and brothers provides, of course, some support for those who answer "no" to the latter question. But increasingly, even religious are becoming engaged in work that detaches them for the most part from their communities and, more than ever then, it is important that they choose the single life.

But returning to the neglect of single Catholics in our parishes, realization of the fact that there is a vocation to the single life, both including and apart from religious celibates, that this is a completely "honorable" vocation, not at all incomplete, might help us to put the single Catholic parishioner in a proper perspective. To assert the integrity of a role for the single Catholic in no way detracts from the dignity of the family. It is important, in fact, to realize that the two roles are not mutually exclusive. The single Catholic, ideally, is a member of a family (or several families) and will sometimes act as part of that family. But single Catholics ought to be full-blooded members of our parishes, their uniqueness recognized, their participation recognized.

Single Catholics need more than their own sets of envelopes and their own index cards come building fund drive time.

Triumphalism Revisited

IT was all in the past, we were told. We Catholics would never be triumphant again. We had rediscovered in the church of the early Christians that ours was to be a pilgrim church. Traveling light always, we would again be open to the world, to other Christians, to non-Christians and to nonbelievers. And as unworthy vessels of the Word, we would be humble. This, more than liturgical changes and modified customs, was to be the heritage of Pope John's council.

Pope who? Old habits are hard to break. Some never die. The other day I saw a photograph taken more than 20 years ago. Four men are posed in front of a kind of throne. In the center, standing on a platform raised perhaps six inches off the level of the others, is an archbishop, whom I know to have been a splendid man and superior leader, complete with ermine cape and full episcopal regalia.

At about the same time that that picture was taken, the Catholic Press Association held its annual convention in Chicago. Even more than it is today, a banquet was the climax of this convention and as the delegates assembled in the banquet room, they found the dais stuffed with 11 bishops in watered silk and taffeta, lace, and with enough pectoral crosses to have turned the tide against the infidels at Lepanto.

The Examined Life

Only one of these bishops was even tenuously a journalist (he was writing his memoirs) but given their preemption, only two places remained for members of the Association. (I was probably traumatized by that experience and if that's what the last judgment is going to look like, I'm not going.)

This morning I participated in a Mass celebrated by a visiting priest whom I have never seen before (I want to make that clear to the priests of our parish). He doesn't homilize, he proclaims. He says, in effect, that the church is not only one, holy, catholic, and apostolic, it is seamless, changeless and definitely unerring. He denounces not Beelzebub or the Albigensians but a priest named Andrew Greeley. After a few snide, certainly unfraternal, personal remarks, he mounts a terribly inaccurate attack on Father Greeley. Meanwhile, the congregation, many of whom undoubtedly practice birth control, sit bewildered while the pulpit orator seems to blame Father Greeley for birth control. He concludes in a flourish of rhetoric, shouting that it was ridiculous for anyone (for heaven's sake, who?) who denied the infallibility of the pope, the virgin birth, and the divinity of Christ to call himself a Catholic. (Now, there's something to warm the hearts of the faithful on a cold, wet Sunday!)

During the week just past, I spent some time at the annual convention of the National Catholic Education Association. I've only been to a few others but this one must have been bigger and better than most.

Robert E. Burns

As far as the eye could see in Chicago's gigantic Mc-Cormick Place, the purveyors of books, audiovisual aids, chocolate bars, fruit cake, and sanitary napkins for use in Catholic schools displayed their wares. Thousands of delegates and visitors streamed through the exhibit area aisles, most noticeably innumerable nuns in habits. (Archbishop Sheen had led me to believe there weren't any such remaining.)

An outsider would find it hard to believe that any American Catholic school anywhere had closed for lack of funds. And if I had been a Protestant, I would have run for my life. I'm sure that one of those exhibitors could have quickly supplied a rack or an Iron Maiden to teach a lesson to any heretic so bold as to intrude on this victory celebration.

At about the same time, the Catholic Press Association released its annual statistical report. The Catholic press, it said, was bigger than ever. Presumably better, but definitely bigger. These figures are undoubtedly as accurate as such figures can be, given the triumphalistic bent of many Catholic publishers, and I can't really fault their release by the Association. It's just that if they imply that all is well in the Catholic press, they're terribly misleading.

And just a week earlier, the press office of the International Eucharistic Congress to be held in Philadelphia that summer announced the names of "the princes of the Church"(!) who would be in attendance.

The Examined Life

Triumphalism, of course, is not limited to Catholics. Dr. Billy Graham and most of the evangelical Protestants play the numbers games to a fare thee well. And a law forbidding triumphalism in advertising would send many a Madison Avenue wizard to the unemployment office.

Some, perhaps many, Americans miss not having a king. Many of the Founding Fathers wanted to crown George Washington. Our most recent former president wanted to dress the White House guard in uniforms copied from *The Student Prince* and is alleged to have been less than pleased if "Hail to the Chief" was not played (or at least hummed) everytime he went to the bathroom.

But isn't it time we all grew up? A mature people and a mature church ought to realize that less is often more, perhaps more often than not. We should not be afraid to be judged, not by our quantity but by our quality.

Pilgrims, it seems to me, are people who know that they haven't "got it all." They know they need to get a lot from God and that they may not ever get it all.

Where Have All
the Children Gone?

QUITE understandably, there is a continuing concern among Catholics, especially Catholic leaders, because of what seems to be an almost total absence of 20- to 30-year-olds at Sunday Mass and other church functions. While this absence may not be a burning problem at the moment, it surely bodes ill for the future. Unless, of course, these wayward lambs return when they get older, but no one that I know of is counting on that.

Various reasons for the defection of the young people have been offered. One distinguished social scientist has declared his belief that the ill-fated birth-control encyclical of Pope Paul caused a loss of credibility in Catholic leadership and this loss in turn led to declining church "membership." Another social scientist, equally distinguished, has recently attributed the defection to the rejection (by young people) of authoritarianism in church leadership.

While I have no doubt that both of these explanations have merit and undoubtedly do explain the defection of *some* young Catholics, I believe that the principal explanation is to be found elsewhere. I have no data to back up my belief (it's off the top of my head) but I wouldn't be offering it here if I didn't think it was true.

Most young people who have severed relations

with the church, temporarily or permanently, have done so, I believe, because they believe the church to be irrelevant. They fail to see any necessary connection between the church and its teachings and their everyday lives. But if this age group finds Catholicism irrelevant, it might be asked, why don't older Catholics feel the same way? Some do, of course, but there isn't any evidence that older (than 30) Catholics are abandoning the church in the fashion of their younger counterparts.

Older Catholics (at least the 40 and up group) tend, I believe, to consider religion a personal, almost private, relationship between God and themselves. In the United States (and Ireland) attendance at Sunday Mass has long been considered the indispensable mark of a "practicing" Catholic. But even at Mass, surrounded by his or her fellow worshippers, the post-40 Catholic, until Vatican II insisted on changes, continued to pray personally and usually silently to "his" or "her" God. Chances are that he prayed that he and his family would be able to lead moral and upright lives or she prayed that she and her family would grow in understanding and love of God. These are valid and laudable kinds of prayer but sadly deficient in concern for the rest of "the people of God," (a phrase that most of us had never heard before the Council and one that we seldom hear today).

Coincidentally (or perhaps fortuitously) with the Vatican Council's insistence that the church must be or become a community, not a collection of praying individuals, many young people began to demand "corporate" morality and "corporate" responsibility for evils such as the pollution of the environment, racism, poverty, and especially the war in Vietnam. Idealistic and perhaps naive young people argued (and more) that "we're all in this together" and that it's up to all of us to do something to solve these problems. Particularly in the late 1960s, the level of consciousness about such social evils rose to astonishingly high levels. But in the church, for the most part, religion and the morality it taught continued to be personal. This limitation may have become more paradoxical because the new liturgy was at that moment emphasizing the church as community and was calling on the worshippers to take responsibility each for the other. I suppose that the relationship of the sign of peace handshake and the immorality of the war in Indochina was bound to seem a little tenuous to Catholics who had for years trained themselves to look neither to the left nor the right at Mass. And the fact that this connection was rarely pointed out by the homilist or in the Prayer of the Faithful didn't help to bridge the gap.

The white heat of moral concern among young people dwindled substantially when the war ended with a whimper. Then came Watergate and another chance for the teaching church to demonstrate that the worst evils in a sophisticated, "civilized" society such as ours are more likely to be social than personal. Few American Catholics would want the church or church leaders to support one political candidate or another. Most Catholics, I am sure, would not want the church to have been involved in presidential campaigns. But not long after the 1972 election, the pattern of Watergate immorality began to unfold and within a year and a half, much of the sordid story had been told. If Catholic leaders or rank-and-file churchmen spoke out vigorously, not against the principals involved in the many Watergate crimes but against the crimes themselves, I'm not aware of this. Such vigorous speaking out would, of course, offer an impressive witness on the part of Catholics in opposition to this kind of social immorality. But it is perhaps even more important that such speaking out would have been powerfully effective catechetically. It would have provided an opportunity for the teaching church to teach, not in a vacuum of theory, but in response to an evil concretely experienced.

I have no way of knowing to what extent the absence of effective witness by the church in the Watergate crisis added to the disillusionment already felt by young people. But the more serious among them could hardly have been blamed if they asked: "What would Jesus have done, were He confronted with such widespread evil? Would He have said, 'Pay no attention to this. Go home and pray for the salvation of your own soul?' Or would He have said nothing and left his followers wondering whether He approved or disapproved?"

Robert E. Burns

Catholic leaders are, I admit, confronted with a Hobson's choice, practically. If they seize the opportunity to teach Christian doctrine by delineating with unmistakable clearness the immorality of the many social evils that surround us, they run the risk of alienating perhaps a majority of several generations of Catholics (generations that among other things do most of the obeying and paying and possibly even of the praying). But if they continue to live with the anomaly that we must have a church so that we can come together to pray separately, I seriously doubt that many of the current younger generation or the generation behind them will return to the fold.

Declaiming Sex

THE Vatican Declaration on Sexual Ethics, not surprisingly, drew considerable attention from the media. Anything that includes the word "sex" seems guaranteed to catch at least a few headlines and to be the subject of more than a few conversations. But the reaction to the Vatican Declaration, both favorable and unfavorable, was really quite mild and anything but pervasive. One need only recall the fireworks that followed the issuance of the papal birth control letter in the 1960s to realize how quiet was the reaction to the recent statement.

Some have criticized the Vatican Declaration but I have no intention of doing that here. Others have questioned the need for such a statement but I don't agree with that criticism either. The Vatican Congregation charged with such matters had apparently received many queries and complaints from various parts of the world asking if the church's teaching in matters of sex had indeed changed. The Declaration was its answer.

Under the circumstances, we could hardly have expected a different set of "answers" than the Declaration gave. But I suggest that the church might have been better served if the Declaration had tried to answer a different set of questions. And because I hope that some day a similar church body will speak out on sex, I boldly offer a few suggestions for its task.

It would in the first place speak about sex and only very incidentally about sex and sin. It would take for granted the fact that *quantities* of sexual sins are committed and it will confront instead the far greater evil that is the debasement of the *quality* of sex. In this context, it would be realized that sex is far more debased by the sophisticated mockery of it on television talk shows than by an adolescent's solitary masturbation. It would recognize that true sex is private, personal and, ideally, unselfish and that we judge whether it has been abused not by asking whether an orgasm has occurred but by asking whether the act has been subverted by selfishness or exploitation.

A truly sound declaration on the subject would, of course, place sex in a human context that includes the intellect, the emotions and the will. (It seems especially ironic that so much of the church's teaching about sexual conduct, or rather sexual misconduct, has made it seem as if the sexual function were an animal function almost detached from the rest of the human personality.)

If we are to have such a declaration from the church in the future, the nature of the deliberative body that will produce the statement is surely important. This body would, in the first place, be composed of both celibates and non-celibates. I am not one of those who believes that celibates have nothing to contribute to a discussion of sexuality. Sexually experienced people, obviously, have a unique contribution to make to any such discussion but their personal experience is often particular and preclusive to universal judgment. It is also often preclusive to humility in a field that more often than not cries out for humble judgment and suspension of judgment.

Perhaps even more important would be the requirement that at least as many women as men be involved in the deliberations. And here again both celibate and non-celibate women should be included. Both men and women ought to be included in any representative group but I would bet that had the church's teaching on sex been handed forth by groups comprised exclusively of women rather than exclusively of men, our history in this area would read far more brightly than it does.

Physical and social scientists ought to be included in our deliberative body but I would not like to see the group overloaded in this direction. I attribute, perhaps erroneously, the peculiar comments on homosexuality in the recent Vatican Declaration to an overweighted contribution from the scientific advisors. Sex, it seems to me, is not a scientific specialty any more than is love or hate or anger or selfishness.

I suppose it might be argued that, given my premises here, it would be better for the church to say nothing at all about sex. But I don't think that that follows logically. The church is and must be concerned about the human condition and sex is a part of (but, mind you, just a part of) that condition. I would like to see the church and everyone else put sex in its proper context, a great good given us by God but no more important than a number of other God-given goods. It is often abused but not nearly so often, I suspect, as some doomsayers would have us believe. It sometimes preoccupies us disproportionately but if it really preoccupied us to the extent that some critics maintain, we would hardly ever get our meals cooked, our clothes washed, our day's work done or even our teeth brushed!

What do you say? Shall we return to "Go" and see if we can do better the next time?

The High Price of Peace

WITH apologies to Mark Twain, peace is something that everyone wants but few are willing to do anything to get. Aside from an occasional, barely aspirated prayer, the pursuit of peace is more often than not left to others.

The Pope (not only Pope John Paul but his predecessors as well) implores not only Catholics but all people of good will to strive for peace. His messages are received with respect, recorded in our media and finally filed and forgotten with no noticeable effect. (Funny how much more attention a papal statement on sex attracts than a papal statement on peace.)

Yet, how can we observe the second great commandment of God that we love one another if we are, practically, indifferent to the cause of peace? Granted that peace in our time has become a terribly complex problem. The day is long past when turning swords into plowshares would put a serious crimp in the aggressive designs of our neighbors or, more recently, when a sizable body of water surrounding a nation would serve to insulate it from predators. But if, despite this complexity, peace isn't possible, we had all better quit taking our breaks at McDonald's and questing for the perfect anti-perspirant and hunker down to await Doomsday.

What, you might ask, can we do to promote peace?

We can, for one thing, begin yelling and hollering about the incredible production and sale of weapons of destruction, an activity in which, sad to say, the United States leads the world. Even with the end of the war in Indochina, our national expenditure for materials of death continues to grow. From time to time, a member of congress or (less often) a president calls for a reduction in our expenditures for military hardware and the systems to deliver it. But when it comes time to vote, they all chicken out. (One U.S. Senator has made a reputation as an opponent of military spending. He delights in finding a proposed program that is patently luxurious or guaranteed to sound silly when denounced on the evening news. But invariably the programs exposed by this vigilant law-maker are budgeted for $100 or $200 thousand and when the time comes to vote approval of the whole, more than a $100 billion war budget, he votes with the overwhelming majority.)

The American people have been frightened into believing that we must stay even with (or better yet ahead of the Russians) in our military expenditures. We are conned into thinking this despite the fact that we have enough destructive weapons to annihilate any enemy a hundred times over. Even a small fraction of our present war-making capability would be threatening enough to deter any enemy from attacking us.

Quite bluntly the argument for military parity with the Russians is so much bilge. Most members of congress and all presidents know this. They continue to

support escalating (and incidentally, almost bank-
rupting) war machines because they haven't the courage to face the voters and say: We can cut our defense
budget in half but a great many people would be
thrown out of work if we did. (For the same reason,
our national leaders waffled last year rather than
take effective steps to sharply reduce the consump-
tion of gasoline. The mere threat of a closedown by
one of the auto manufacturers sent our "leaders"
scurrying for cover.) Supposing our congress and
presidents had the courage to bite the military-
spending bullet (and they might if enough of us told
them that's what we wanted) and declare at the same
time that the government of all the American people
would become the employer of last resort. Everyone
able to work would be given a job. Which would be
preferable, spending $50 billion to provide jobs or
spending $50 billion to manufacture ever more hid-
eous weapons of death? Weapons of death that, once
on hand, someone will sooner or later find an excuse
to use.

Beyond the chilling stockpiles of weaponry we continue to build for ourselves, there is a smaller but still
awesome quantity of weaponry that we manufacture
and sell (or give) to other countries to conduct their
own wars. (The phrase "their own" has become a
black-comical term now that nuclear weapons are
almost at the fingertips of even the smallest nations.)

We aren't especially choosy as to whom we supply
weapons. In a number of "war theaters," most nota-

bly in the Middle East, we supply weapons to both sides (what in name of God is that supposed to accomplish?). The quality of the government a nation receives doesn't seem to have anything to do with whether we supply arms to them, either.

Sadly, the UN is in a terrible mess. It is still, probably, better than nothing but the line that divides utility from utter futility for the UN seems to have come ominously close. Far too many UN members, including our own, seem to be playing domestic politics in that international body that began with such high ideals and hope. (Ironically, the urge to bounce every UN debate and vote off the folks back home seems to cut across all ideological positions. The Russians, the Israelis, the Nigerians, and the Americans seem equally to be playing for the people in Minsk, Tel Aviv, Lagos, and Peoria.)

But whatever (if anything) we as Christians choose to do to promote peace, we surely must start with our obligation to love one another. If we do not start here, we will inevitably bog down in the sophisticated argumentation that the new warmongers try to confound us with. Our obligation to love one another ought to be the touchstone by which we answer the questions, "Should we do this?" or "Should we do that?" Without such a touchstone, we are likely to be no match for Dr. Strangelove.

Bishops' Move

THE only (elected) living former President of the United States continues to give us the benefit of his wisdom. In one interview he deplored the growth of cynicism among the American citizenry. (That's a little like Jack the Ripper denouncing the timidity of the London burghers who wouldn't let their daughters go out after dark.) But in answer to those who charge that I never give Mr. Nixon credit for anything, let the record show that I agree with one statement of his in the interview. "Our religious leaders," he said, "are failing to give us leadership."

This comment by the former president isn't likely to go down too well with the prominent religious leaders who prayed in the White House during his incumbency and stayed for breakfasts of eggs and toadyism. But it's hard to gainsay.

Coincidentally, the Catholic bishops of the United States were holding their annual meeting in Washington when Nixon's criticism was voiced. And once again, as they have in almost every recent year, the bishops failed to say anything of any real significance to American Catholics or to Americans in general.

Much time, apparently, was devoted to the abortion question and it's hard to object to that except to say: Is there anyone who doesn't already know where the bishops stand on abortion?

Robert E. Burns

A package of resolutions on the American economic situation (calling for full employment, better health and other assistance for the poor, etc.) was approved but that could hardly have been a surprise to anyone.

The UN attack on Zionism was deplored and "the dialogue with women" (what a grimly sexist phrase!), it was vowed, would be continued.

Perhaps we shouldn't expect anything more from a convocation of 300 bishops. I say this sincerely and without any sarcasm. Perhaps we should be happy that they aren't thundering anathemas and excommunications and that their statements are as meek and mild as they are. But is this leadership?

I know only a handful of the American bishops (and those not well) but I am under the impression that individually they are virtuous men who are deeply concerned with the spiritual and moral well-being of the people "charged" to them. Granted that many of them have been chosen for their administrative skill rather than for charisma, I find it hard to believe that many of the 300 do not have genuine qualities of leadership and could not, given the opportunity, offer creative solutions to widespread problems, particularly future problems.

So, what happens when these individuals merge to meet in annual conclave? Well, for one thing, a few aggressive bishops take charge. (One-third of the floor time at the November meeting, we are told, was monopolized by a single bishop with many opinions of his own.) For another, the American bishops, unlike their European and Canadian counterparts, tend to be "company men" who think it best "not to make any waves." "To get along," the late Sam Rayburn advised U.S. Congressmen, "go along."

On some subjects the bishops are obviously restrained by their lack of special competence. Most of them recoil in horror when a subject such as homosexuality is raised because it is eons away from their experience. But no one expects the bishops (or indeed other leaders) to be expert in every specialized field. As at the Second Vatican Council, the voices of experts in particular fields should be listened to.

But I think the shortfall of the bishops' meeting is, more than any of these weaknesses, a tendency to react rather than to act. It is the habit of the bishops assembled to chase after problems that are already here rather than to try to anticipate problems of the future. One bishop at the recent meeting called on a committee of the group to act as a "watchdog" to guard the faith that he felt was being eroded. What a pity that a similar convocation ten or twenty years ago hadn't tried to build in the health of the American Church rather than treat its "illnesses" after these were ingrained.

Leaders, after all, are almost always out in front. Rarely are they barking commands from the rear or nipping at the flanks. (The sole exception to this rule may be the dogs used to herd cattle and sheep.)

Many Catholics, particularly lay Catholics, seem

to have little interest in things episcopal because they fail to see what any of this has to do with their individual Catholic lives. And in the blessed absence of the "anathemas and excommunications" that once were hurled from episcopal thrones, they may be right. But creative leadership from the bishops, the kind of leadership that I see signs of in individual bishops almost every week, could change all that. Perhaps it would help if individual bishops would realize that once a bishop they can't be fired. (In the immortal words of Ira Gershwin, "oh, no, they can't take that away from me.") Barring heresy or scandal (which God forbid), what may very well be the silent majority of American bishops ought to make its voice heard. I can't help feeling that they have a lot to say that is worth saying and that with the help of the Holy Spirit at least part of our religious leadership vacuum might be filled.

Religious Snobbism

ON a bus one day in Italy one of our fellow passengers was an American of Italian ancestry who didn't seem too enchanted by the land of his ancestors until we reached Padua. There in the Basilica of St. Anthony, our fellow passenger found the shrine dedicated to the city's patron. The sides of the shrine were almost covered with hundreds of petition slips as well as notes thanking the saint for favors received. Our fellow passenger was enchanted and revived when he saw this because, I gathered from his remarks, he was at home with this cultural expression of religious faith. And who has a right to say he was wrong?

In the days when many of us thought that the liturgical movement was the greatest thing since apple butter, it was fashionable to laugh scornfully at the pious ladies who banged their (usually oversized) rosary beads against the front of their pews during Mass. While saying the rosary is obviously inappropriate during Mass, I wonder how many of the critics of the pious ladies could honestly say that they were participating in the liturgy with any more concentration and devotion than were the beads-sayers.

It has also become fashionable in some circles to decry prayers of petition. Let's get rid of "gimme prayers," we are told. But those who say that suffer

from astigmatic vision also. Some of the most significant prayers in the public life of Jesus were just such
"gimme prayers." ("If it be your will, Father, let this
chalice be taken from me." or "Give us this day our
daily bread.") and a lot of people praying prayers of
petition may be asking, "Gimme the grace to lead a
good life."

I remember an article in a Catholic newspaper
which juxtaposed a picture of a large office-ware-
house used by a religious organization for some questionable fund-raising work and a photo of a votive
light stand. In view of the fact that nothing in the text
of the accompanying article mentioned votive lights,
readers should be excused if they inferred that there
is something not quite kosher about votive lights.

Now obviously votive candles or lights aren't for
everyone. There's no reason why they should be. But
it's one thing to disdain votive lights and quite
another to disdain people who reverently use votive
lights to express their devotion and trust in God.

I am sure that some, perhaps many Catholics, who
have grown up in the almost bloodless, Anglo-Saxon
tradition of metaphysical or "spiritualized" religion
would be appalled were they to stumble on the annual
San Gennaro street festival so common in Italy and
in many American cities with sizable Italian-Amer-
ican populations. In some places, of course, this
celebration has become far more secular than religious. But the religious motivation at the center of
the festival hasn't been entirely lost in the carnival

welter of singing, dancing, eating, drinking and, I suppose, even wenching.

Far more religious but almost as colorful is the celebration of the feast of Our Lady of Guadalupe in many places by people of Mexican ancestry. Bright costumes, even brighter music of mariachi bands, accompanied in the not-too-distant past by the singing of many caged canaries.

It may be a hangover of our Puritan heritage that causes some of us to frown on any emotionalism in the practice of our religion. Even more, though, it is, I think, the heritage of an immigrant church that, anxious to be more American than the Americans already here, acted out this urge to be more restrained (a critic might say "suppressed") than the prevailing Anglo-Saxon, Protestant Church.

More recent generations of Catholics, more extensively educated than their parents and grandparents, have tended to look down their noses at religious practices that are less than cerebral. Some of these are easily embarrassed by devotional practices that they consider "old country" or sentimental. And surely they have every right to exclude such practices from their own devotional lives. But the charity that should hold members of a religious community together should preclude the kind of harsh judgment or smartass rhetoric that is a mark of the religious snob.

There is an awful lot of room in the Catholic Church. We ought not to turn it into an elite, exclusive club.